CHRISTIAN HE~~~~~EN & NOW

KLAUS-DIETER JOHN

Hope in the Land of the Incas

To Kim

love Jo~~~

CHRISTIAN HEROES: THEN & NOW

KLAUS-DIETER JOHN

Hope in the Land of the Incas

JANET & GEOFF BENGE

YWAM
PUBLISHING

P.O. BOX 55787   SEATTLE, WA 98155

YWAM Publishing is the publishing ministry of Youth With A Mission (YWAM), an international missionary organization of Christians from many denominations dedicated to presenting Jesus Christ to this generation. To this end, YWAM has focused its efforts in three main areas: (1) training and equipping believers for their part in fulfilling the Great Commission (Matthew 28:19), (2) personal evangelism, and (3) mercy ministry (medical and relief work).

For a free catalog of books and materials, call (425) 771-1153 or (800) 922-2143. Visit us online at www.ywampublishing.com.

Klaus-Dieter John: Hope in the Land of the Incas
Copyright © 2014 by YWAM Publishing

Published by YWAM Publishing
a ministry of Youth With A Mission
P.O. Box 55787, Seattle, WA 98155-0787

First printing 2014

Library of Congress Cataloging-in-Publication Data
Benge, Janet, 1958–
  Klaus-Dieter John : hope in the land of the Incas / Janet & Geoff Benge.
     pages cm.—(Christian heroes, then & now)
  Includes bibliographical references.
  ISBN 978-1-57658-755-3 (pbk.) — ISBN 978-1-57658-634-1 (e-book)
  1. John, Klaus Dieter—Juvenile literature. 2. Physicians—Peru—Biography—Juvenile literature. 3. Missionaries, Medical—Peru—Biography—Juvenile literature. I. Benge, Geoff, 1954– author. II. Title.
  R472.J64B46 2014
  610.92—dc23
  [B]   2013043797

Printed in the United States of America

CHRISTIAN HEROES: THEN & NOW

Available in paperback, e-book, and audiobook formats.
Unit Study Curriculum Guides are available for select biographies.
www.ywampublishing.com

Peru and Ecuador

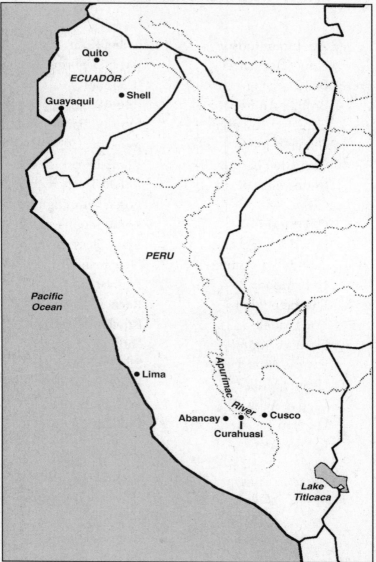

Contents

Chapter 1

Future Jungle Doctor

Klaus turned another page of his book and continued to read.

> Then I found a definite swelling behind his ear. We went outside. I took Daudi by the arm. "We have to do it, and do it now. This is a job of which I've always been frightened."
>
> "Why, Bwana?"
>
> "You're operating perilously near his brain. There's a very big sort of vein right in the middle of the bone we have to chisel out, and also, Daudi, I've never done this operation before."

"Time for me to go to bed," Klaus's father, Rudolf, said as he appeared in the doorway of his son's tiny bedroom. "A good book?" he asked.

Nine-year-old Klaus nodded. *"Jungle Doctor Operates.* This is the best one in the series so far. You should read about how God helped him get back to the hospital during a flood, and how the men arrived just in time to save a bleeding woman. They weren't supposed to be on that road, but God told them to go there just when Dr. White was needed. And now he is about to operate close to a boy's brain!"

Rudolf John smiled. "Yah," he said. "Thank God for men like Dr. White. The stories he tells take place thousands of miles away in Africa, but it is the same God we serve. We can trust God to guide us and protect us wherever we are. Isn't that wonderful?"

"Yes, it is," Klaus said. "Good night, Papa. I hope work goes well for you tomorrow."

Klaus listened as his father shut the bedroom door and went to say good night to his brother, Hartmut. His two older sisters, Gerlinde and Helga, were talking quietly in the living room next door. Soon Klaus heard his father walk down the hallway to his room. It was eight o'clock, and Rudolf would go to bed now and be up at 2:00 a.m. ready for work.

Sometimes, if Klaus happened to awake during the night, he would hear his father getting dressed and the top step creaking as Rudolph slipped downstairs to the bakery. Directly below Klaus's bedroom was the old stone oven. Klaus recognized every sound—the shoveling of coal into the fire below the oven, the bread pans being loaded into the oven to cook, the snap of the oven door as it closed, and the thump of the bread being turned out onto the counter when it was done baking.

The bakery on Rhein Street belonged to the John family, and Klaus had lived there since his birth in 1960. One of his earliest memories was of being lifted onto a stool in the corner by the big bakery oven. Klaus had watched his father knead bread dough, roll it, cut it, and place it into greased pans. His mother told him that he had started asking his father questions that very day and never stopped. It was true. Klaus still loved to sit on the stool and talk while his father worked.

Although Rudolf had never been to university, every night he read for an hour before bed. He could talk knowledgeably about Germany, politics, religion, and history. While Klaus loved to hear him talk about such things, most of all he loved it when his father told stories about his childhood—stories of growing up in a wealthy family in Silesia in eastern Germany, where they had owned a bakery and farm before the war. All had been well until the 1930s, when Adolf Hitler rose to power. Klaus's father's family watched this turn of events with alarm. The John family was devoutly Christian and belonged to the Brethren Church. They had been loyal supporters of Kaiser Wilhelm and did not like Adolf Hitler or his ways at all. Yet they knew it was dangerous to protest too loudly.

In September 1939, when Klaus's father was fourteen years old, Germany invaded Poland, beginning what would become World War II. In 1944, when he was nineteen, Rudolf John was drafted into the German army. As he fought, he continually prayed that God would help him survive. In the winter of 1945, at the age of twenty, he was injured and taken to a military hospital. While he was in the hospital, Germany surrendered and the war ended.

After his release from the hospital, which had been captured by American soldiers, Klaus's father, along with thousands of other German soldiers, was handed over to the French and taken to a prisoner-of-war camp at Lille, on the border between France and Belgium. Thousands of men were held there in open fields surrounded with barbed wire. They had no coats or blankets and very little food. They ate grass and drank the water from foul puddles. Every day hundreds of men died from starvation and disease.

At Lille, Klaus's father realized that if he did not escape, he too might die. So he made a plan. Sometimes the prisoners were hired out to help local farmers, and Klaus's father volunteered for the job. Rudolf often told Klaus about the night he escaped. He was being housed on the second floor of a farmhouse along with three other prisoners. Vicious dogs guarded them at all times.

In the middle of the night, Klaus's father crept out of bed, tied his sheets together to make a rope, and gently opened the window. The whole time he prayed that the watchdogs would not bark. Down the sheets he slid, still praying. There was no noise inside the house, and the dogs remained silent.

When he reached the ground, Rudolf put on his shoes and ran for the woods. Because it was far too dangerous to travel in daylight, he had to walk at night and hide during the day. He estimated that he would have to walk nearly two hundred miles across

France and Luxembourg to get back to safety in Germany, and he had no idea how long it would take him to cover that distance. All he had to eat during this time was "soup," which he made with water and flour.

A French soldier with a dog caught sight of Klaus's father a few days into his journey to freedom. Rudolf ran for cover and hid in a clump of bushes. He thought he might evade the soldier, but the dog would easily smell him. Klaus's father prayed fervently and watched as the dog approached the bushes, sniffed, and moved on. The soldier became frustrated and began to curse the dog, leading it back to the bushes. But the dog could not pick up the scent and continued to sniff in a different direction. Eventually the soldier hauled the dog away, still cursing. Rudolf breathed a prayer of thanks as he slipped deeper into the woods.

"You see, Klaus, God never leaves us alone," Klaus's father would say at this point as he recounted the story of his escape.

After two weeks Rudolf reached the Luxembourg border, but crossing it was no easy task. Soldiers were stationed all along the road at the border. As Klaus's father hid behind a rock and surveyed the scene, he noticed that one soldier smoked almost continuously while staring toward the mountains. Praying as he went, Rudolf inched his way toward the border. As he moved along, the soldier remained with his back to him, facing the mountains and drawing on his cigarette. Even when Klaus's father was so close that the soldier could have reached out and touched him, the soldier did not turn around. On went Rudolf John, aware that if anyone saw him, he would be shot where he stood. The seconds ticked by as he made it safely across the border into Luxembourg. Before long he arrived at the Mosel River, which formed the border between Luxembourg and Germany. He forded the river at a shallow spot where he'd observed smugglers crossing. Weak and hungry, Klaus's father finally made it back to Germany.

The Germany that Rudolf returned to was vastly different. The country was now divided among the Allies into French, Russian, American, and English zones. Everywhere Rudolf looked, he saw bomb damage, with many buildings turned into nothing more than piles of rubble. Klaus's father always had tears in his eyes when he told about what had become of his country.

Unsure of where to go, Rudolf eventually headed for the city of Wiesbaden, in the American zone. He hoped that he would find work there while he decided what to do next.

As he set out for the railway station and the train to Wiesbaden, a car pulled up beside him and a stranger asked, "Where are you going?"

"To the railway station," Rudolf said.

"Let me give you a ride," the man said.

Klaus's father was pleased to save the little energy he had left by not having to walk to the station. When they arrived there, the man reached into his pocket. "Here, let me give you some money," he said, handing him twenty reichsmarks before driving off.

Rudolf was speechless. Just twenty minutes before, he had set out on foot for the railway station with no money for a train ticket, and now he was at the station with money in hand. The twenty reichsmarks just covered the cost of a ticket to Wiesbaden. This was another reason to thank God, Klaus's father always pointed out when he retold the story.

When he arrived in Wiesbaden, Rudolf found work in a bakery. One job led to another, and two years later he applied to a bakery closer to where he lived. The baker was impressed with his knowledge of bread making and agreed to hire him. Klaus's father wanted to make one thing clear before he accepted the job. "I have to tell you, I am a committed Christian," he said, "and I pray before all my meals. Will that be a problem for you?"

"Oh, we are used to that," the baker replied. "There is a Baptist girl working here who does the same thing."

That girl was Wanda Reinsch, and she had a gripping story of her own to tell. Wanda was from a devout Baptist family from Pomerania, also in the eastern part of Germany. When the Russians took control of that region, her family realized they could not stay there. The family piled what they could of their belongings into horse-drawn wagons and joined a grim caravan of Germans heading west. Russian airplanes shot at them from above, and many of the refugees were killed. Wanda, her parents, eight sisters, and one brother prayed constantly as they fled. Finally, they made it safely to the American zone, where they settled in Wiesbaden. Once in Wiesbaden, Wanda took a job working in the bakery.

During 1949, as Klaus's father continued working at the bakery, Germany was divided into two countries: the Federal Republic of Germany, which consisted of the western two-thirds of Germany, and the German Democratic Republic, which occupied the third of the country occupied by the Russians at the end of the war. The Federal Republic of Germany, or West Germany, as it was mostly known, was free and democratic and had a capitalist economy. The German Democratic Republic, or East Germany, was a Communist state under the control of the Soviet Union and—as Klaus's father liked to point out—was anything but free and democratic.

Working together at the bakery day after day, Wanda and Rudolf became friends and prayer partners. In 1953 they were married.

Klaus found it hard to imagine his parents as daring young people, one fleeing her home while being attacked by Russian airplanes, and the other creeping past guards with machine guns to escape to safety. Klaus's own life seemed so normal and predictable in comparison. But one thing he knew for certain: he would not spend his life as a baker in a town in Germany. No—he already knew that he was going to be a missionary and lead a daring, adventure-filled life of his own. The Jungle Doctor books he loved to read showed him this was possible, as did the many missionary slide shows he saw at church on Sunday nights. The chapel wall would pulse with images of missionaries fording rivers, driving up steep mountain passes, or motoring across the African savanna in trusty station wagons, luggage roped to the roof and wild animals loping alongside. That was the kind of life for Klaus!

Chapter 2

A Test of Faith

One fall afternoon, ten-year-old Klaus walked home from school with his friend Michael Schubert. As they walked, Michael seemed quiet to Klaus, and it wasn't until they turned onto Rhein Street that he finally spoke up. "Klaus, my mother says I can't hang out with you anymore or go inside your house."

Klaus turned to face his friend. "What do you mean? What has happened?"

Michael shrugged. "Remember last month when I went to church with you and gave my heart to Jesus?"

Klaus nodded. How could he forget?

"Well, I didn't tell my mother, but I started reading my Bible, just like your father said I should. She saw me and asked what I was doing. I told her I was now a follower of Jesus, and she got very angry. She said it was all nonsense, that you and your family had put silly ideas in my head, and that I can't see you anymore."

Klaus was shocked. He knew his family was viewed as an oddity in Wiesbaden. The Johns were members of a Baptist church that everyone called "Kapelle." It was a tiny, misunderstood denomination in Germany. Most Germans were more comfortable with the teachings of the two state-sponsored churches, the Catholic church and the Lutheran church.

"Do you think she means it?" he finally asked Michael.

Michael nodded, looking miserable. "I'm sure she does. I tried to talk to her about it this morning, but she says I have to get all this strange religious stuff out of my head, and the only way that will happen is if I stay away from you."

Klaus didn't say much more. He knew that Michael's mother had a temper and it would be useless arguing with her.

When he got home, Klaus put his satchel in his room, shut the door, and opened his Bible. He was looking for a particular verse, one that Pastor Cassens had preached on the Sunday before. Using the concordance at the back of his Bible, he found what he was looking for in the eighteenth chapter of the Gospel of Luke. Verses 1–8 told the story of a woman who needed something from an unjust judge. Klaus read the verses aloud to himself.

Then Jesus told his disciples a parable to show them that they should always pray and not give up. He said: "In a certain town there was a judge who neither feared God nor cared what people thought. And there was a widow in that town who kept coming to him with the plea, 'Grant me justice against my adversary.' For some time he refused. But finally he said to himself, 'Even though I don't fear God or care what people think, yet because this widow keeps bothering me, I will see that she gets justice, so that she won't eventually come and attack me!'" And the Lord said, "Listen to what the unjust judge says. And will not God bring about justice for his chosen ones, who cry out to him day and night? Will he keep putting them off? I tell you, he will see that they get justice, and quickly."

When he had finished reading the verses, Klaus got down on his knees and prayed. "God, this story says that You hear our prayers, and I am praying to You now and asking that You make Michael's mother change her mind so that he can play with me again and come to church with our family. Amen."

With that, Klaus stood up, placed the Bible—opened at the story—on his desk, and went downstairs to help his father. It was Klaus's turn to accompany his father as he made the late-afternoon bread deliveries in his Opel van. Klaus knew what needed to be done. He had been delivering bread with his father since he was eight years old. First they loaded the bread, buns, and other specialty baked items—this time of year they were plum cakes—onto the shelves in the van. Then they drove around the city making deliveries to the homes of customers.

As they drove down Kahlemühle Street, Rudolf turned to Klaus and said, "You are very quiet today, son. Did school go well?"

Klaus nodded. And this was true. Klaus was always at the top of his class in every subject, and he also excelled in most of the sports he tried.

"Is there something else?"

Klaus did not answer. He thought of the open Bible on his desk and decided that he would leave the matter to God. He wanted to test his faith and see how God would answer his prayers.

When the deliveries were over, Klaus still had an hour before dinner. He went upstairs to his bedroom. Most of the other boys in his class watched television after school, but the John family did not own one. "When would we watch it?" Klaus's father would say, and his mother would nod and reply, "It's better for the children to be studying than watching cartoons."

Klaus began his English homework. It was confusing trying to learn word order in English. In German there were several ways to put a sentence together, but Klaus's English teacher was always reminding Klaus to use S.P.O.—subject, predicate, object—and it was hard to get it right all the time. To make matters worse, Klaus could not pronounce the English "th" sound. This was the last of the speech problems he'd had since he was a small child. Over time a speech therapist had helped him to pronounce German words correctly, but English was a new challenge, as so many words had "th" in them.

Every so often, as Klaus worked on his studies, he remembered Michael and glanced over at the open Bible still on his desk. "God," he said aloud, "You said You would hear my prayers. It says so right on this page. I want to play with Michael again and take him to church. I am counting on you to change his parents' minds."

One day passed, and then another. Klaus watched for Michael after school, but his friend walked home by a different route, and the two boys did not see each other. Then, on the third day, Klaus spied Michael running to catch up to him. "It's okay now," Michael said, beaming. "I don't know what happened, but this morning my mother told me not to worry about what she'd said. I can play with you again!"

Klaus let out a whoop of joy. He had his best friend back. Better still, he had trusted God to fix the situation and it had all worked out, just like it had in the story of the widow and the unrighteous judge.

The following year Klaus and Michael attended different schools. Klaus had won a place at the Elly Heuss High School, a school for thirteen hundred top students who were studying to go on to professional careers. Klaus quickly rose to the top of the class, despite the fact that he was now expected to get up at 5:00 a.m. every other morning to help his father bake bread. At 7:30 on these mornings, he took a quick shower, gathered his books, and ran all the way to school, often eating a roll as he went. Klaus fell asleep many times in class, but he dared not tell his parents, who believed in working hard and helping out the family.

In spite of the demands at home, Klaus also ran the *Jungschar-grupp*—the boys' club at church. He loved the outdoor activities the most: the treks through the woods and the nights spent around a campfire telling stories. Klaus particularly enjoyed the challenge of keeping every boy listening intently to what he said.

As a natural athlete, he also excelled at table tennis, swimming, rowing, and long-distance running. On the outside Klaus looked as if he had everything going for him, but he had one big problem: he was haunted by a fear of dying. Sometimes he wondered whether it came from worrying about his father. As a young boy, Rudolf John had suffered from diphtheria, a bacterial infection in the upper respiratory tract, and had been blind and paralyzed for a week. Everyone around him at the time had prayed hard. Rudolf recovered, but the doctor warned him that the sickness had damaged his heart, and he would be lucky to live to be forty. Klaus's father told the story of his diphtheria to show how God can heal people, but Klaus could not stop thinking about how his father might die soon. Then he began to worry that he too would die. Klaus's imagination turned every headache into a brain tumor and every sore into a cancerous growth. These nagging doubts about his health were hard to cope with, especially since he knew that he would be laughed at if he expressed his fears to anyone.

Klaus's fear of death, though, drove him to dig deeper into his Christian faith. Other boys his age did not want to think about Christianity, but to Klaus it felt like a matter of life or death. He had to know whether it was true or not, and sooner rather than later.

During 1977 Klaus had a unique opportunity: he was selected as one of three students to represent his high school on a television quiz show called *Die Sechs Siebengescheiten*. It was a huge honor, since over five million people tuned in on Friday nights to watch the show. Klaus had to chuckle to himself. Ordinarily he would not be one of those five million people, because his family still did not own a television.

The quiz show allowed each student to choose his or her own topic on which to answer three questions. For as long has he could remember, Klaus had been fascinated with Jewish history, so he chose that as his topic. A busload of students accompanied him to the city of Baden-Baden, where the quiz show was filmed. Klaus and his teammates were taken backstage while everyone else filled the front rows. The show started. Klaus adjusted his tie. The honor of his high school was at stake, and he did not want to let everyone down.

Klaus was relieved when the announcer asked the first question, which was on Masada, the ancient fortification located atop an isolated rock plateau on the eastern edge of the Judean Desert, overlooking the Dead Sea. He gave the correct answer, and the audience clapped enthusiastically.

The host then asked the next question. "What was the year the Jews returned to Israel from captivity in Babylon?"

"538 BC," Klaus replied.

Again the audience clapped.

The host then asked the third question. "What was the title of the book Theodor Herzl, founder of the Zionist Congress, published in 1896?"

"*Der Judenstaat,*" Klaus answered.

Again the answer was correct, and the audience let loose with thunderous applause. Klaus had answered all three of his questions correctly.

The other two students representing his high school also got their questions right, and by the time the quiz show was over, Elly Heuss High School ranked first place in the contest. Klaus was proud that his team had won the amount of twenty-two hundred marks for their school.

The next year, when Klaus was seventeen years old, he got to see Israel firsthand. He signed up for a seventeen-day tour with seventeen other Christian youths. He had earned the money for the trip working at the bakery and at McDonald's flipping hamburgers. He hated the McDonald's job, but every week he watched his bank account grow until it was large enough to pay for the trip. During the seventeen days, the tour crisscrossed Israel, from the border with Lebanon to the Red Sea. It was an amazing experience. Having listened to countless Bible stories at Sunday school and church, now Klaus actually got to see where Moses had parted the Red Sea and where John the Baptist had baptized Jesus. As the tour bus stopped to see the place where Jesus had preached by the Sea of Galilee, Klaus knew it was worth all his hard work to get there. It was an experience he was sure he would never forget.

In 1978 Klaus started his second-to-last year of high school. He knew he would have to work hard to earn a place at a top university where he could study medicine. He'd already decided to become a doctor, even though several of his teachers urged him to consider becoming a politician.

On the first day of class, Klaus was arranging his textbooks in his bag when he heard a girl chatting and laughing. The girl had a beautiful voice. He turned around to see a young woman with long, curly brown hair. She turned to look at him with the bluest eyes Klaus had ever seen. Klaus thought to himself, *Who is she? Why haven't I run into her before?*

Much to his surprise, Klaus soon learned that this mystery girl, Martina Schenk, was in most of his classes. He tried to talk to her but soon found that the two of them had little in common. Tina, as everyone called her, was a Lutheran who went to church once a year—at Christmas—and thought anyone who went more often than that was a fanatic. She talked about how much she loved to dance, how she went to discos every Saturday night, and also how she took ballroom dancing lessons and was working toward a gold medal in that. Klaus could not relate to that at all. German Baptists thought dancing was evil and to be avoided at all costs. And listening to the girls around her talk, Klaus realized that Tina lived in a social whirl—horseback riding one weekend, partying with friends the next. It was so very different from his orderly life that revolved around study, church, and family.

Still, Klaus was attracted to Tina and kept trying to talk with her to find things they had in common. Even he was shocked at a conversation they had one afternoon. Very matter-of-factly, Tina announced, "When I graduate, I'm going to medical school to become a doctor, and then I am going to work in a Third World country to serve the poor."

Klaus paused. "Really, Tina? You honestly mean that?"

Tina nodded.

"That's exactly what I'm going to do too!" Klaus exclaimed. "How long have you wanted to do that?"

"For as long as I can remember," Tina said with a smile.

That night Klaus could hardly sleep. He could not get the conversation with Tina out of his mind. Tina was everything he wanted in a girlfriend—strong, opinionated, popular, and very smart—but she was not a Christian. Tina might be the most popular girl in the senior class, but she would not meet his parents' approval. Yet Klaus could not give up on the idea of getting to know her better. Somehow there had to be a way to work things out.

Before long Klaus and Tina were spending time together. They made an agreement. One Saturday night they would go to the disco with Tina's friends, and the next Saturday they would go to the church youth group. Just as they predicted, neither set of parents approved of the situation. Tina's parents warned her that the Baptists were a weird cult that would take over her life if she was not careful, and Klaus's parents urged him to date one of the girls from church. Yet somehow Klaus and Tina made the relationship work.

It did not take long for Klaus to realize just how much he hated discos. The thumping of the music was ear shattering, and the pulsating lights were too bright. Klaus couldn't understand why Tina and her friends loved it so much.

Just as Klaus was getting discouraged about the dating arrangement, Tina confided in him that she really liked attending the youth group. Eight months earlier, she had fallen off a horse and broken her pelvis in several places. Spending six weeks in recovery lying on her back in the hospital gave her plenty of time to think about death and the meaning of life. She had come away with far more questions than answers, and the talks at the youth group were helping her think things through.

Soon Klaus was elected joint high school president, along with his two best friends, Alex Peuker and Reinhard Dörner. Tina became coeditor of the school newspaper. Since Klaus was on the student leadership council, he and Tina got to see each other at many different events as well as in class.

Tina excelled academically during her final two years of high school. She passed a series of exams and interviews and was awarded a scholarship from the Deutsche Studienstiftung, a government foundation that honored the top one percent of high school seniors in all of West Germany.

In 1980 Klaus and Tina graduated from high school and applied to the same medical school at Johannes Gutenberg University located in Mainz on the other side of the Rhine River. As he walked through the corridors of Elly Heuss High School one last time, Klaus thought about how many more years of study he had to go. He was now nineteen years old, and he would be twenty-six before he would be Dr. Klaus-Dieter John.

By now he was sure that Tina would be his wife and his partner throughout life. Just weeks before, Tina had attended an evangelistic tent meeting in a nearby town. She had listened to the preacher and been very impressed with his honesty. The preacher had spoken of how he and his wife had had a child who died, adding that he still believed God was there with him in the midst of tragedy. Tina told Klaus that when the preacher invited people to come to the front and accept Jesus Christ, she had stepped forward. From now on, she assured Klaus, she would forget the discos and spend all of her Saturday nights at youth group with him.

Klaus was delighted with Tina's decision to become a Christian. This was something he had prayed for every day since meeting and falling in love with her. The way ahead seemed bright and clear. They would get their medical degrees and head out to serve God together—at least, that's what he hoped.

Chapter 3

Premed

Klaus prepared for a long year of study. He moved out of his parents' home and into his own apartment nearby. It was a big move, and now he was totally dependent on himself. He had to do his own washing, ironing, and cooking. He soon came to appreciate everything his parents had done for him.

The school year started in April 1980, and both Klaus and Tina enrolled in premed classes at the university in Mainz. Gerlinde, Klaus's oldest sister, had just graduated from the school and was embarking on a career as an elementary school teacher. Hartmut, Klaus's brother, was in his third year of studying English, Latin, and history, while his other sister, Helga, was two years ahead of him studying accounting. Klaus seldom saw them, as the campus of Johannes

Gutenberg University was so large. While keeping up with his coursework, Klaus also kept busy coleading the church youth group with Tina.

As the first set of university exams approached, Klaus focused on his studies. Open books and papers were scattered on every surface of his tiny apartment, and he read through them and reorganized them a hundred times. He did not even take the time to wash his dishes, and a small plant soon began to grow in his kitchen sink. Klaus's mother was not impressed when she came to visit, but Klaus wasn't concerned. He had to get top marks in his exams, and he did.

During the first half of the summer of 1980, Klaus and Tina made money working for a market research company. Every morning they reported to an office in town to get their orders. Sometimes they walked up and down the main street, clipboards in hand, stopping people and asking them whether they preferred red or gray cars or whether they liked the lettering on a particular cereal box. Other times they met with groups of people—focus groups—and asked them questions about the products they bought and what they thought of them. It was interesting work, and Klaus learned a lot about how to talk to people from all walks of life. The money was good too, and by August, Klaus and Tina had earned enough to pay the rent on their two apartments for the next few months and still had enough left over to pay for an adventure.

In mid-August, Klaus surveyed his red Renault and declared the car fit for a road trip—all the way to England. Tina's father was not so sure. The Renault was old and rusty, so rusty, in fact, that it had holes in the front floor, allowing the driver and passenger to see the road beneath. Tina's father welded metal plates onto the floor to stop things from falling out and things on the road from coming into the car.

With the repairs made, the two set out on the nine-hundred-mile trip. Their first stop was Frankfurt, where they joined ten other young people from a Baptist youth group. In all, they had three cars among them, including Klaus's Renault. They drove through Belgium and on into northern France, where they caught a ferry from Calais to Dover, England. From Dover it was a 120-mile drive north to Bedfordshire, where the annual Greenbelt Christian Music Festival was to be held.

Being at the Greenbelt Festival was a dream come true for Klaus. He loved Christian music and had collected more than a hundred record albums. For four days he and Tina enjoyed the fellowship and sat on the grass of the Odell Castle grounds with about twenty thousand other Christian young people from all over England and Europe. They clapped their hands to the beat as Larry Norman, Randy Stonehill, Cliff Richards, and others performed. It felt wonderful to Klaus to be with such a diverse group of Christians. In fact, it was hard for him to leave the festival when it was over, and he promised himself that he would return the following year.

The trip back to Wiesbaden proved to be an eventful one, as pieces of the Renault began to fall off along the way. At one stage the muffler tumbled to the road and had to be tied back in place with a piece of fencing wire.

Despite his car slowly falling apart on the journey back, Klaus made it home safely and was soon back into his hectic schedule. He continued to study hard and passed all of his exams, as did Tina. The two of them saw each other often, since they were study partners, youth group coleaders, and had the same friends in common.

The pattern of the first summer at university was repeated over the following summers. Klaus and Tina got jobs, saved up their money, and headed to England to the Greenbelt Festival. It was just the combination of relaxation and faith-building music that Klaus needed to keep him going throughout the coming year of study.

Everything was running along smoothly until spring 1983, when Tina came into the university cafeteria bursting with excitement. "I have something to tell you," she told Klaus, putting down her cafeteria tray next to his. "Something amazing."

"Don't keep me waiting," Klaus said.

"You know the six-week internship we have to do in spring?"

"Yes," Klaus said.

"Well, I'm off to Ghana for it!"

"In Africa? That Ghana?" Klaus queried.

Tina nodded, her eyes shining.

"But isn't it politically unstable? This morning I read in the newspaper that there has been a failed coup and the country's leader, Jerry Rawlings, is

clamping down on anyone who had a part in it."
Klaus thought for a moment. "And isn't that where
people are starving to death as well?"

Tina nodded. "You're right. Ghana has a lot of
problems—but what an opportunity. I can't miss
it! Chris Sackey says it will be fine. He's helped me
find contacts. I keep telling you I want to work in the
developing world, and this is my chance to try it out.
Aren't you excited for me?" Tina asked.

Klaus barely nodded. He had a feeling Chris
would somehow be involved. Chris was studying
economics at the university and was one of the few
African men on campus. Klaus liked Chris, but he
wasn't thrilled about Tina traveling to Ghana.

"What did your parents say?" Klaus asked, hoping they might be able to dissuade Tina from going.

"They think I'm crazy," she said. "They'll adjust.
Somewhere along the way they are going to have to
accept the fact that I'm not going to stay in Germany
and earn tons of money. My heart isn't here. I think
they are beginning to understand that."

Klaus nodded. If Tina wasn't going to listen to her
parents, she certainly wouldn't listen to him.

For the next two weeks, Tina spoke of little else
besides her trip to Ghana. She told Klaus how she was
in touch with Monika Yeboah, a German woman who
had married a Ghanaian doctor who studied in Germany and now lived in Ghana. Monika had offered
to find a hospital where Tina could do her internship.

Klaus continued to try to convince Tina not to go,
but Tina proved to be as stubborn as he was. Klaus

visited the office of the Ministry of Foreign Affairs and asked for information about visiting Ghana. The man behind the desk shook his head. "Not a good idea," he said. "Can't you find somewhere safer to go sightseeing?"

"It's more like a hospital mission trip," Klaus said.

"In that case, if you must go, make sure you register with the German Embassy in Accra as soon as you arrive. We are trying to keep tabs on everyone in the country, though there's probably not much we can do if you get yourself into trouble out in the countryside. Where are you going in the country?"

Klaus shook his head. "Actually, it's not me. It's my friend. She's not sure where she's going, but she hopes to spend time in a large city hospital as well as a small village clinic."

"Good luck with that," the man said. "Tell her to register as soon as she gets there and report in with her whereabouts. That's all the advice I can offer you."

Klaus read a lot of newspaper articles about conditions in Ghana. Things were not going well in the country. More than a million Ghanaians had been expelled from Nigeria, and their arrival back in Ghana had only made conditions in the country worse. Ghana was in the grip of a severe drought, and the place was politically unstable. To make matters worse, the Ghanaian government had just introduced an economic recovery program that had made life even more miserable for the poor, while the country's middle class were fleeing as fast as they could.

The more Klaus read, the more worried he was about Tina.

After chemistry lab one day, Klaus and Tina walked back to the library together. "Are you sure you still want to go?" Klaus asked, reeling off the many things he had read and then adding, "People are being kidnapped and killed there. The man at the Ministry of Foreign Affairs said it's a bad idea to travel there—that you should find somewhere safer to go."

Tina nodded. "I know it's not the safest place to be," she finally agreed, "but I always said I wanted to work in a developing country, and this is a great opportunity to see whether I am cut out for it. Lots of places in the world aren't guaranteed to be safe all the time. I feel like God wants me to go."

"In that case," Klaus declared, "I think I should go too. We both want to work in the Third World. Let's go see what it's like together."

Tina smiled. "Okay. I wondered how long it would take for you to tag along."

That weekend Tina and Klaus drove to Tübingen to meet with an elderly Catholic nun named Dr. Marquard, who had spent twenty-five years in Ghana. Dr. Marquard welcomed Klaus and Tina into her home, where she served them bread and hot tea. Over the course of an hour, the doctor explained some of the problems of medical work in Ghana. The hospitals were poorly equipped, and the standard of care was low compared to Germany. There was also a lack of basic understanding about hygiene among the people, and this led to the rapid spread of infectious diseases. Dr. Marquard warned Klaus and Tina that they would be shocked by the living conditions in Ghana and that they would encounter many cultural differences.

When it was time to leave, Dr. Marquard handed Klaus and Tina some boxes of malaria tablets and read Psalm 91:7 to them: "A thousand may fall at your side, ten thousand at your right hand, but it will not come near you."

On the drive home Klaus and Tina were silent. The reality of going to a politically unstable, famine-afflicted country was setting in. Klaus kept repeating the verse to himself as he drove. For the first time he was going to test his calling to be a doctor in the developing world. He did not feel brave and full of faith about what lay ahead. In fact, he felt quite the opposite—he was scared.

Chapter 4

A Waste of a Good Medical Education?

On August 25, 1983, the Tupolev aircraft touched down on the runway in Accra, Ghana. Klaus unbuckled his seatbelt and stood up. It had been a long, tiring trip. To get the cheapest tickets available, he and Tina had booked an Aeroflot flight that went from Frankfurt to Moscow, then on to Odessa, to Tripoli, and finally to Accra.

Klaus and Tina collected their overhead bags, headed up the aisle, and stepped out into the African summer. The humidity engulfed Klaus at the doorway. He stepped down from the airplane and walked across the tarmac and into the terminal building. A sea of black faces peered at the couple. Klaus took a deep breath. He was overwhelmed at seeing so many faces staring at him. As he wiped sweat from his forehead, Klaus wondered whether coming here had been the right thing to do.

"The customs and immigration lines are going fast," Tina said as they lugged their bags across to the final inspection point.

"That's because we're about the only foreigners coming in," Klaus replied. "Anyone with any sense is getting out of Ghana."

Tina gave him a nudge. "Klaus, we will be fine. Remember the verse Dr. Marquard gave us. God is with us."

"*Akwaaba*—welcome!" Klaus heard the words and looked across the crowd to see a hand waving at him. It was Chris Sackey. Soon Chris was slapping Klaus on the back and asking whether he and Tina had had a good flight. Several other burly men stood nearby, watching their every move.

"I have a van waiting," Chris said.

"I have to use the bathroom first," Klaus replied.

"Me too," Tina echoed.

Chris pointed to the left and maneuvered them through the crowd in that direction. As Klaus entered the bathroom, he was struck by an overwhelming stench. When he opened the door of a stall, he discovered sewage overflowing from the toilet bowl onto the floor. Klaus gagged, shut the stall door, and opened the next one. Again his senses were assailed with the same sight and smell. In fact, every toilet in the men's bathroom was overflowing. Klaus had no choice but to use one of them anyway.

Klaus waited for Tina to exit the women's bathroom. When she did, she looked grim.

"Pretty bad?" Klaus asked.

"Yes, pretty bad. I guess we really are in the Third World. I just didn't expect it at the airport . . ." Tina's voice trailed off, and Klaus knew she was thinking about how much worse things might be in the poor areas of the country where they were headed.

As they drove out of the airport, Klaus saw a line of cars parked right along the roadway. The line seemed to be about a mile long, and no drivers were in sight. Chris saw Klaus staring at the line of cars. "No gas," he said. "It's almost impossible to get any. They run out of gas waiting for the gas station to get some in."

Despite the fact that few vehicles were on the road, they moved slowly. So many people were milling around that it was hard for Klaus to take it in. Crippled children sat on grass mats begging for food, while old men with missing arms and legs shuffled across the road. It looked to Klaus like something out of an end-of-the-world movie set. When they came to a roadblock, men in uniforms swarmed the van.

"Just keep quiet. I'll handle this," Chris said, flashing Klaus and Tina a big smile.

Klaus sat silently and watched from the window as a soldier pointed his gun at an old man up ahead. The man fell to his knees, his hands raised in surrender. Klaus was close enough to see the panic in the old man's eyes. The soldier prodded the man's back with the barrel of his rifle and yelled something. Klaus held his breath, praying that the old man would not be shot.

Meanwhile, a soldier barked in Ghanaian for the van to move forward. The driver waved and drove off. Klaus looked behind. He was relieved to see the old man struggling to his feet as the soldier spat on the ground and walked away.

On just about every street corner they passed, Klaus saw groups of men squatting on the pavement. "What are they doing?" he asked Chris.

"Playing dice games."

"Don't they have something better to do?" he inquired.

Chris shook his head. "The women do most of the work in Ghana. They tend the fields and raise the kids. The men hang around a lot."

Klaus's thoughts flashed back to Germany, where his father got up at two o'clock in the morning to bake bread and worked hard all day before sweeping the bakery floor and closing up shop in the late afternoon. From an early age, Klaus had been taught the value of earning what you received. Now he was confronted with men who played dice all day long and expected their wives to put food on their plates. People had warned him before he left Germany that he would experience culture shock, but he didn't anticipate the disgust he felt at the way the men behaved. He sat grim-faced, staring out the window, thinking. *Perhaps the developing world was not the place for a hard-working German man, after all.*

Klaus and Tina spent two nights in Accra, adjusting to the time change and getting accustomed to the stifling humidity. Then it was time for them to head to Kumasi, where Monika Yeboah lived. The city of Kumasi was about 150 miles northwest of Accra, and Chris had promised to secure seats for them on an airplane headed there. When they arrived at the airport, Klaus wondered whether they would be flying that day. The flight information board showed that most flights had been canceled, and people were arguing with the ground staff, pushing children toward closed doors, and yelling as they waved parcels in the air.

Even though Klaus did not understand the Ghanaian language, he could see that most of the people were hoping to get on the same plane as he and Tina. There was no way they were all going to fit.

In the chaos, Chris handed Klaus a letter. "This is from the Secretary of Health. Hand it in with your ticket. It says that the bearers of this letter must be admitted onto the first available flight to Kumasi."

"Will it work?" Klaus asked.

Chris smiled a big, white-toothed smile. "That is entirely up to you, my friend. How fast can you run?" He chuckled, but Klaus remained stoic. "This letter will get you through those doors and out into the fenced area on the tarmac. From there on it's up to you. When the gate opens, run as fast as you can to the steps of the airplane. They will count passengers getting onto the plane, and when it's full, they shut the doors."

Klaus nodded grimly. It was so different from the orderly boarding process in Frankfurt when they had left Germany.

Sure enough, after showing the letter, Klaus and Tina got through the preboarding process and were soon standing with hundreds of people in the enclosure on the tarmac. The sun beat down on them, babies started to cry, and children played clapping games together. In front of them was an airplane being readied for flight. Klaus looked at the crowd of people waiting to board. There was no way that more than half of them could be seated on the plane. He felt bad for those people who, after waiting so long, would not get a seat. After three hours, a voice on the loudspeaker announced that the plane was boarding. Klaus gripped his bag in one hand and grabbed Tina's hand with the other. They sprinted through the open gate and across the tarmac, passing many people encumbered with odd-sized packages and small children. Breathlessly, they reached the steps and climbed into the airplane.

As Klaus settled into a seat, he witnessed the last few people struggling onto the plane. As the steps were pushed away from the fuselage, he heard loud wailing outside and realized that many parents and children had become separated. The aircraft door was quickly closed, and a hostess walked up and down the aisle shoving bags and packages into lockers and under people's seats.

As the airplane's engines revved for takeoff, Klaus looked out the window. He was not sorry to be leaving Accra. He thought of the words he would use to describe his experience of Africa so far—smelly, disorganized, dirty, overcrowded. He let out a sigh. It was depressing to think about how quickly his missionary zeal had evaporated when confronted with a real Third World situation. *Getting out of the capital city will help,* he told himself as the plane took off. *Kumasi will be much better.*

Monika and her children welcomed Klaus and Tina into their home. It felt good to be in a clean, orderly place again. Monika poured them glasses of pineapple juice and quizzed them on how things were back in Germany.

Klaus and Tina's six-week internship was very flexible. It was meant to be a time for medical students to learn by observing the practice of medicine in other settings and, where possible, to put into practice what they were learning in the classroom. The following day, Monika dropped Klaus and Tina off at Anokye Hospital, where she had arranged a tour for them. As Klaus entered the hospital, he noticed a peculiar smell. He looked at Tina, whose nose was crinkled up at the odor.

Klaus and Tina walked through the hospital, shocked by the conditions. The building was run-down and underequipped. The wards were open, with dirty curtains dividing the beds. All around, patients screamed and wailed, the noise reverberating down the corridors.

An hour later, Klaus and Tina were sitting in on the doctors' daily meeting. Klaus had a sinking feeling as he listened to the topic for the day—how to get rid of the rats in the hospital. *So that was the strange odor.* Klaus tried not to show his revulsion at there being rats in a hospital, but his imagination ran away with him. Rats could gnaw on immobile patients. They could spread deadly diseases through their droppings and eat through wires and tubes hooked up to life-saving machines.

After the meeting, a nurse was assigned to walk Klaus and Tina around the hospital grounds. As they walked, Klaus noticed groups of people sitting or standing as if they were waiting for something to happen. "Why are they here?" Klaus asked.

The nurse shrugged her shoulders. "Waiting for money, I suppose," she replied.

"For money?" Tina chimed in.

"Yes," the nurse said. "See that building near the gate? That's the supply shop. We assess a patient's condition and then provide them with a list of what they will need before we will admit them. It's their job to buy the items and bring them back so that they can be admitted into the hospital and start their treatment."

Klaus frowned. Surely he had misunderstood. "Say I had a broken leg. What would I have to buy?"

The nurse looked surprised, as if Klaus should know better. "The list would include anesthetics, bandages, and plaster."

"And patients have to buy all that over there and bring it with them to the emergency room or you won't do anything for them?" Klaus pressed.

"Yes," the nurse said.

Klaus kept his mouth shut, but barely. He was having trouble imagining an accident victim having the time or the resources to buy a long list of medical supplies before being admitted to the hospital.

Later, as they walked out through the gates, Klaus could see a few fortunate people with bags filled with medical supplies, but many others were sitting or standing nearby with forlorn looks on their faces. One man who begged him for money lifted his shirt to show Klaus a plastic bag that, as far as Klaus could tell, contained his intestines. How they had ended up on the outside of the man's body he could not imagine.

The following morning Monika took Klaus and Tina to a pediatric clinic run by Dr. Hunter, an Indian man. Tina was particularly excited, as she had decided to become a pediatrician. As the car pulled up to the clinic, children surrounded it. Some had their hands out, begging for money, while others just stood staring at the tall, white people who got out and walked inside the cinderblock clinic building.

Inside, Dr. Hunter sat at a wooden table with an empty seat to his left and a notebook to the right. A bell rang, and the nurse who had been outside brought in the first round of children. Klaus and Tina watched as one by one the children lifted their tops and sat down in the chair. Dr. Hunter grasped each child's belly with his left hand while writing notes with his right hand.

"I feel the liver with my fingers and the spleen with my thumb," he said, looking up at Klaus. "Ninety percent of these children have malaria. I can tell right away if the organs are enlarged."

The line of children stretched out the door and around the corner. By the end of the morning, Dr. Hunter had seen over two hundred young patients. "That's it for now," he told the nurse. "Time to switch to my other job."

"Your other job?" Klaus asked.

Dr. Hunter nodded. "Yes, keeping the clinic open. I have to go out and get supplies—paper, pens, gas, and food. If you don't organize these things yourself, you will have to manage without them in this political climate. You can't rely on the locals to help you. They might never come back. If I want something done correctly, I have to do it myself."

Klaus turned to Tina. He knew she was thinking the same thing.

That evening, sitting on the veranda outside Monika Yeboah's house, Klaus and Tina had time to talk. Just as Klaus thought, Tina was also disturbed by what they had seen.

"It's awful," Klaus said, sucking the juice from an orange. "And the rat smell. I'm not sure I'll ever forget that. Rats in a hospital! Can you imagine that in Germany? And having to do all the administration work just to keep your clinic open. Think of how many more patients you could see each day if you didn't need to do all that yourself."

Tina laughed nervously.

Klaus picked up another orange. "Here's what's worrying me," he began. "Why would a person train for ten years in one of the most sophisticated medical colleges in the world and then come over here to work, where the equipment and treatment are so antiquated, even barbaric? It seems like a waste of a good medical education, don't you think? I mean, we are learning theory and using state-of-the-art equipment, and here they don't even know what to do with those things. Anyone who has taken a basic first aid course can make a difference here."

The two medical students sat in silence. Klaus was not even sure he wanted to go back to Anokye Hospital or the pediatric clinic for a second day. At dinner that night, Klaus talked to Monika about how disillusioned he was.

"God will direct you," she said. "Just keep praying and asking for help, and He will show you the way ahead. The Bible says He knows every sparrow that falls to the ground, so He surely has His eye on you and your future."

Klaus nodded. It would be rude to tell his hostess that he thought she was a little too naive. *Yes*, Klaus told himself, *I do believe in God, and I do believe God wants me to be a doctor. But this idea that God directs everything that happens to me—perhaps I'm getting a bit too old to believe that.*

Late the following afternoon, Monika invited Klaus and Tina to visit Dr. Eldryd Parry, professor of medicine at Kwame Nkrumah University of Science and Technology in Kumasi. Professor Parry was a tall, spindly man who spoke English with a lilting Welsh accent. In contrast to their visit the day before, Klaus and Tina found this visit uplifting. Professor Parry had been a Christian for many years and had given up the possibility of a lucrative medical practice in England to serve the people of Africa. He had written a book on tropical diseases and been awarded an Office of the Order of the British Empire (OBE) by Queen Elizabeth II for his efforts. Klaus talked to the professor about what he had seen. Like Monika, Dr. Parry urged him to have faith and press on with his plans.

By the time the conversation with the professor was over, the sun was setting. "I'm so sorry," Monika said as the three of them got back into her car. "It's nearly six. I had no idea it was this late. The curfew starts in five minutes. We'll have to pray we make it back safely through the checkpoint."

Klaus gulped. It didn't sound likely to him. On the way to Dr. Parry's home, they had passed a large checkpoint manned by well-armed soldiers. All Klaus could think of was the old man being forced to his knees by a soldier near the airport in Accra the day they arrived. The soldiers liked to show off their weapons in Ghana—that was for sure.

Soon it was totally dark. All the lights in the city were turned off, and there were no street lamps, no neon signs, no extra lights in shop windows. Klaus also noticed that theirs was the only car on the road. How would they slip by the checkpoint if they were the only ones on the road?

"We need to start praying," Monika said. "We're only a street away. God is with us."

Klaus glanced at Tina, whose eyes were shut and lips were moving. Suddenly he heard a thunderous crash, then saw a bright flash of light as the night exploded into a tropical storm. Monika turned the corner. The checkpoint was barely visible in the driving rain. Klaus peered through the darkness to see the soldiers sprinting back to their hut. Monika drove on, passing the barbed-wire fence and the guardhouse, and headed on down the road.

"That was incredible!" Tina exclaimed. "The rain came at just the right moment. The soldiers didn't even care about us. They were too concerned about keeping dry."

"See?" Monika said cheerfully. "If we commit our plans to God, He takes care of the details."

Klaus nodded but still had nagging doubts. Was it just a coincidence that a downpour had occurred at the exact moment they needed a distraction, or did God really care about every little detail in his life?

A week later, Klaus and Tina found themselves sitting on the veranda of the Methodist Medical Clinic on the shores of Lake Bosumtwi, about twenty miles southeast of Kumasi. A no-nonsense British nurse named Marjorie manned the clinic.

"Of course, malaria is one of the main problems," Marjorie told Klaus and Tina as she took a bite from a scone. "I have four Ghanaian assistants, and we treat between fifty and eighty patients a day. The clinic has its limitations. We dress wounds and dispense medicines, things like that, but we don't have a doctor to operate. Births are a problem, too. Some of the local women act as midwives, but if things go wrong, the nearest hospital that could do a cesarean section is miles away. We've lost a few mothers and babies lately . . ." Her voice trailed off.

They all sat in silence for a minute or two. Then Marjorie changed the subject. "While you're here, you must walk around the lake. It's almost a perfect circle—a crater lake. Forty villages are dotted around the edge."

"How long would it take to walk?" Tina asked.

"About a day," Marjorie replied, "but it's well worth it. You'll see the real Africa out there."

The next day Klaus and Tina set out early to walk around Lake Bosumtwi. Klaus felt as if he were in one of the Jungle Doctor books he had read as a child. Undulating hills surrounded the lake, and nestled between them and the water's edge were sleepy fishing villages made up of straw-roofed round huts. Flat-bottomed canoes were pulled up along the shoreline, and round nets hung from poles, drying in the sun. Children scurried around while women stirred large pots over open fires. The dull pulse of drums floated across the lake. Klaus expected the Jungle Doctor himself to step out of one of the huts at any time. Everything was perfect, except for the constant chirping, buzzing, and biting of insects.

The sun was setting as Klaus and Tina returned to the clinic, and they watched the sky turn from gold to scarlet and then to purple. Klaus thought he'd never seen a sunset so beautiful.

The next morning Tina had a high temperature and aching bones. She had contracted malaria. Now Marjorie had one more patient to care for. Under her care, Tina was up and about again in several days. In the meantime, Klaus helped out at the clinic. He was impressed with Marjorie's compassion for the local people but disturbed by the number of very ill patients who had to be turned away because the clinic could not do anything for them.

After two weeks at the Methodist Medical Clinic, it was time for Klaus and Tina to leave Lake Bosumtwi. Klaus was sorry to go. Life there was such a tranquil contrast to Kumasi. Klaus dreaded returning to the city. It was depressing to think of the dirty streets and the deformed beggars sitting among piles of trash. Klaus wished he could just get on an airplane and fly straight home. He was over the whole idea of being a missionary doctor in a developing country. It was just too much work for too little return. As far as he could see, you worked either in a better-equipped government hospital where no one seemed to care whether the patients lived or died or in a small, well-meaning Christian clinic with virtually no equipment and little medicine.

Professor Parry invited Klaus and Tina to stay with him on the last night in Ghana. As Klaus lay awake thinking about his time in the country, images flooded his mind, such as the man who had gotten up from playing dice to beg for money. "Tell them we need help over here. Send us money," the man had said. Klaus couldn't resist snapping back, "God helps those who help themselves. Stop playing childish games and do something useful!" Before coming to Africa, Klaus could not have imagined himself saying something like that. No, Africa—or at least Ghana—was not what he had imagined it to be. As a result, rather than wanting to serve in a Third World country, Klaus couldn't wait to get back home to tidy, clean, and orderly Germany. He wondered how a man like Dr. Parry could keep going day after day, week after week, serving an endless stream of diseased and dying people while never giving the impression he felt taken advantage of.

As Klaus drifted off to sleep in his upstairs room, he heard Professor Parry singing in the room below, and not radio hits but psalms from the Bible. As Klaus lay there listening, tears began to stream down his cheeks and onto the pillow. Below him sat an older man—a brilliant man—who had given his life for the people of Africa, living through all the problems, the lack of equipment, the surly staff, the rat-infested wards, the ungrateful patients, and who was still happy. Klaus knew this was because he drew his strength from his faith in God. Eldryd Parry had not allowed unanswered questions or unmet expectations to derail or defeat him.

For the first time Klaus understood clearly the choice ahead of him. He could either let the problems he had encountered discourage him and make him give up his plans of working as a doctor in a developing country or embrace the idea that God was in control and would be with him through all the problems he encountered.

"Blessed is every one that feareth the LORD; that walketh in his ways. For thou shalt eat the labor of thine hands: happy shalt thou be, and it shall be well with thee." The words of Psalm 128 drifted up through the floorboards as Dr. Parry sang. Klaus smiled to himself. On the very last night of his six weeks in Ghana, he had found the key that would allow him to carry on. He would follow Professor Parry's example of humble service and continue on God's path.

Chapter 5

In America

It was a Sunday afternoon in January 1984, and Klaus sat in his room at home in Germany. He could have been outside enjoying the crisp, sunny winter's day, but he had more important matters to attend to.

Since arriving back from Ghana, Klaus had been dogged by the idea that God wanted him to do his final year of study in the United States. Unable to shake the notion, he decided to make a list of what it would take for this to happen. On the left side of the paper in front of him he wrote down all the reasons why it would be difficult to study in America. On the other side he listed ways he could improve his chances in each area. It took him half an hour to write the list:

Why it would be difficult	What I can do about it
Don't speak good English	Find a place to practice English
Different blocks of study times	Pray
Cost of traveling/studying is higher	Take on extra jobs
Don't have connections in the USA	Pray
No idea where to apply to	Find catalog of US universities
Might lose touch with Tina	Pray

Now that he had a list, Klaus could see what he had to do. He would apply to the US Air Force hospital at Wiesbaden to do a block of training there—that would help improve his English, particularly English medical terms. He would be on the lookout for extra ways to earn and save money, and he would request a catalog of American universities that had medical schools. As for the other three items, he would do the one thing he could think of to do—pray. So right then and there, he got down on his knees and closed his eyes. "God, if You want me to study in America, please show me how to make it happen. I need help with all the steps I have to go through. Please guide me and take care of everything by the first day of my exams in August next year."

When Klaus got up, he was confident his prayer had been heard. He had recently read a quotation from Saint Augustine: "Pray as though everything depended on God. Work as though everything depended on you." That was the way forward. Klaus would do everything he could to get to America and pray every night that God would make it happen.

The next day Klaus set about putting his plan into action. He sent away for a catalog and applied to the

Air Force hospital for a placement. He also bought a copy of The Living Bible in English and started reading his way through it. And every night he worked on the prayer part of his project.

A month later the catalog of American universities with medical schools arrived. The catalog listed 120 universities Klaus could apply to. Since it was too early to begin the process, Klaus placed the catalog on his desk next to the atlas of the United States and laid his hands on both of them as he continued to pray each night.

One year later, Klaus was still praying every night. He had done everything he could, including an internship at the US Air Force hospital at Wiesbaden and taking on extra jobs to save money. He had researched every university in the catalog until he'd narrowed the list of 120 universities down to 40 that appeared to be possibilities. He translated his résumé into English, made forty photocopies of it, and sent them off to the universities. In Germany, the final year of medical school consisted of three four-month block placements: one in internal medicine, one in surgery, and the third in a specialty. Klaus requested his four-month placements in the United States.

Meanwhile, one of the other things that Klaus had been praying about each night was not going so well. Tina had broken up with him and was now dating his best friend, Reinhard Dörner. Reinhard was a brilliant physics student with a bright academic future. Klaus felt lost without Tina. He had been sure they would get married and go to the mission field together.

Klaus continued to pray nightly and now searched the mailbox daily, but nothing came from the universities. Then finally, letters began to arrive. Klaus opened each one eagerly, but his spirits soon fell. "We regret that we are not able to accommodate your request . . ." "We do not have a program that is compatible with the German model you describe . . ." "We have very limited spaces for overseas students, and they have already been filled with applicants who better fit our criteria . . ." The wording was different, but each letter was always the same—no one wanted to take responsibility for the last year of study for a German medical student.

Finally, two universities did offer a glimmer of hope. The University of Wisconsin offered him a two-month training block in surgery, and the University of Texas offered an eight-week placement in gynecology, but neither would be available until 1986. Klaus needed something that started in October 1985. Besides, the schools were offering two-month placements, when he needed four months. Still, every night he continued to pray. "God, if it is Your will, take me to America."

In July, with the end-of-the-year exams fast approaching, Klaus was summoned to the dean's office for a meeting. It was not a pleasant experience.

"So when are you going to give up on this silly idea of studying in America, Klaus?" Professor Löffelholz asked.

Klaus wanted to say that it was a silly idea only if God was not behind it, but he lost his courage. "I just need a bit more time. I haven't heard from all of the schools I applied to in the United States yet," he replied.

The dean frowned and rearranged some papers on his desk. "Time is the one thing you don't have. If you do not wish to stay enrolled at this university for your senior year, you need to tell us what German university hospital you wish to study in. Studying in the United States is obviously not going to happen. You do not have even one four-month placement in America. Can I be any clearer than that?"

"No, sir," Klaus mumbled.

"You have until tomorrow," the dean said as he stood and showed Klaus to the door.

As he walked out of the dean's office, Klaus had absolutely no idea what to do next. He had done exactly what the quotation from Saint Augustine had said to do. He had prayed and worked—now what?

That night Klaus sat on his bed feeling depressed and defeated. Then a thought came to his mind: *Ask God for an acceptance letter in tomorrow's mail.* Klaus did not know where the thought came from, but he felt a sudden surge of energy. Quickly he knelt and prayed, "God, if You are there and if it is Your will, send me an acceptance letter from the USA in the mail tomorrow."

The next morning Klaus could hardly wait for the mail delivery. As soon as he heard the mailman, he ran downstairs. His hands trembled as he opened the mailbox. Inside was one letter—with a US stamp on it. He ripped it open and read. It was from Case

Western Reserve University in Cleveland, Ohio, and said, "Mr. John, we are pleased to inform you that we are able to offer you two months' training in surgery."

Klaus stared at the letter, reading it again and again. Yes, it was true. Case Western had accepted him for two months of study in October, 1985!

Without going back upstairs, Klaus jumped into his car and headed for the university. Professor Löffelholz needed to see the letter. Klaus held it in his hand as he walked into the dean's office. "I have been accepted by Case Western Reserve University for two months' training in surgery," he said triumphantly.

The dean read the letter carefully, a surprised look on his face.

"And I have been offered a two-month placement in surgery at the University of Wisconsin. Together with this, that makes a four-month placement," Klaus pointed out.

Professor Löffelholz sat and thought and then said, "All right. It is unusual to do it this way, but I will grant you an exception. You can go and study at these two universities in America. But may I remind you that to graduate you must also organize placements in internal medicine and a specialty practice."

Klaus could hardly believe what he was hearing. This was a complete turnaround from the day before—the dean was going to let him study in the United States after all. And while he had to work out his internal medicine and specialty practice placements, Klaus was certain God would take care of this for him as He had the surgery placement.

Two weeks later Klaus received another letter, this time from the University of Virginia, offering him the opportunity to study internal medicine for four months. His internal medicine placement was now taken care of.

Then on the first day of his end-of-year exams, the exact day Klaus had spent a year and a half praying toward as his deadline, he received one last letter—from the University of Denver, inviting him to train in pediatrics for three months. Klaus let out a whoop of joy. All his prayers had been answered. With these and the eight-week placement in gynecology at the University of Texas, Klaus had a year's worth of training in the United States. It was time to get out his atlas and see where Cleveland, Ohio; Madison, Wisconsin; Richmond, Virginia; Denver, Colorado; and Houston, Texas, were located.

The two months following the exams were a whirl of activity as Klaus prepared to spend a year in the United States. He bought a plane ticket, packed his suitcases, and said good-bye to Tina. Even though they were no longer dating, Tina promised to write to Klaus, who hoped she would. It was difficult for Klaus as he got on the airplane, remembering how the two of them had gone to Ghana together two summers before. Klaus prayed silently, asking God to take care of him and Tina and the different paths they had chosen.

On October 25, 1985, Klaus flew into New Jersey. He spent several days in New York City with his old school friend, Axel Peuker, who was now a consultant to the World Bank. From New York, Klaus flew to Cleveland to begin his American medical training at Case Western.

Klaus soon learned that although the American medical training system was different from its German counterpart, it was every bit as grueling. He was expected to sign in at the Metropolitan Hospital every morning at 5:00 for a round of patient visits and consultations with an experienced doctor. Then he would assist with surgeries for the rest of the day. Every third evening Klaus was assigned night duty, which meant he worked all day, all night, and all the next day before getting a break. He also had hours of classes to attend. Klaus was not the only medical student who sometimes fell asleep during lectures. It was impossible to keep up a 120-hour workweek without collapsing from exhaustion at some point.

Much to Klaus's delight, Tina wrote to him each week, filling him in on what she was up to and how their friends were doing. She did not write much about Reinhard, which suited Klaus fine. The fact that they were dating was still a sore spot with him.

The two months in Ohio sped by, and soon after Christmas Klaus took a Greyhound bus to Madison, Wisconsin, to start his next block of training in surgery. He could not believe how cold it got in the United States in winter. A thick blanket of snow covered everything, and even sipping hot coffee from a paper cup did not make him feel warm.

Once again, Klaus settled in easily to his new situation. The workload was tough, but apart from going to church on Sunday mornings, Klaus did not have any social obligations. At the University of Wisconsin he was placed under the care and tutelage of Dr. Mack, a very competent surgeon. Klaus felt comfortable with the doctor and soon confided in him that he had a secret hope of going to Harvard Medical School while he was in America. Much to Klaus's surprise, Dr. Mack jumped on the idea and sent off a detailed report on Klaus's work to the famous medical school. He included a cover letter stating that Klaus would like further training, as he intended to be a missionary doctor one day.

Klaus was still waiting for an answer from Harvard when it came time for him to leave Wisconsin and head to his third block of training at the medical college at the University of Virginia in Richmond, where the weather was considerably warmer than in Wisconsin.

Once in Richmond, Klaus noticed that he was the only student from Europe studying there. One day, when he was turning in some paperwork, he struck up a conversation with one of the administration officers. "I wonder why I was chosen," he said. "Did you by chance have anything to do with the selection process?"

The officer grinned. "As a matter of fact, I did. I'm afraid it's not very scientific. Each year we get hundreds of applications from Europe, and most of the applicants are qualified to study here. There is no way to pick the best candidate, so to be honest, I just stuck my hand into the pile, and yours was the application I picked out. Everything looked in order, so you became our first choice."

Klaus smiled to himself. What were the chances of his letter being picked out of a pile like that? He said a quick prayer of thanks for his improbable acceptance to the Medical College of Virginia.

Douglas Palmore was assigned to be Klaus's advisor in Virginia, and he, too, took a special interest in Klaus's dream of going to Harvard Medical School. He wrote a letter of recommendation to Harvard, and within a few weeks Klaus had his answer—he had been accepted into Harvard Medical School for not one but three surgery electives at Massachusetts General Hospital in Boston, the primary teaching hospital of Harvard.

Before heading to Boston, Klaus went to Denver and then to Houston to complete the other placements he had been offered.

Klaus received more good news. Tina wrote to say that she had broken up with Reinhard and planned to visit Klaus in the United States as soon as she graduated. Encouraged by Klaus's experiences, Tina had arranged an elective for herself at Boston City Hospital. By early spring 1987, Klaus and Tina were both in Boston, though they worked at different hospitals.

While in Boston, the two of them took a week off to travel to Martha's Vineyard. It was there that Klaus asked Tina to be his wife. She agreed and told him that although she'd had a great time with Reinhard, she felt she would be throwing away her dream of being a doctor in developing country if she married him. It was clear to her that Reinhard's life revolved around cultural events—the theater, dance, operas, charity balls. It would be a good life for some woman, but not for Tina. In saying yes to Klaus, Tina knew that she was also saying yes to the life of a missionary doctor.

The couple wanted to get married as soon as possible and left the United States to return to Germany in May 1987. Their wedding date was set for August 1, 1987, and Tina set to work making wedding plans. For Klaus the day could not come soon enough.

More Training

Following their wedding, Klaus and Tina moved into a tiny loft apartment on the west side of Wiesbaden. Klaus was now twenty-six years old and well on his way to becoming a distinguished doctor. He had studied at six American universities and earned nine certificates of honor in various areas of medicine along the way. Nonetheless, Klaus, who now wanted to be a surgeon, decided to do additional study in surgery for a doctorate degree, while Tina decided to so the same in her specialty, pediatrics. Both of them felt that being specialists would one day be useful in developing countries.

In August 1988—one year after their wedding—Klaus and Tina completed their doctoral studies. Klaus had passed his German Medical Exam, and both of them had traveled to Frankfurt for the American Foreign Graduate Medical Exam. They both passed, meaning they could now practice medicine in Europe and the United States.

The question then became what to do next. Neither of them felt they should stay in Germany to practice medicine or return to the United States to do so. Instead, Great Britain seemed like a good choice to further their medical training. Under the British training program, young doctors changed jobs often, learning from each new placement. This approach appealed to Klaus and Tina.

The Johns were both accepted into the British medical training program and were soon busy working at a university clinic in Cardiff, Wales. From there they went to work at clinics in Leicester, then Leeds and Bolton, and finally Manchester. Life was hectic, and sometimes Klaus and Tina went for days without seeing each other. Yet they knew they were receiving vital medical experience. They also liked the atmosphere of Great Britain. Klaus found the British to be more friendly and helpful than the Germans. Despite this, he and Tina also felt it was time for a new challenge, and they began to pray about moving to the United States for further medical training.

In the summer of 1990, Klaus sent out application packets to seventeen US universities, seeking a residency position in surgery. Much to his delight, he was accepted at Yale University's teaching hospital in New Haven, Connecticut. Now that Klaus had a position, Tina began applying for a residency at teaching hospitals near Yale. The best offer she received was to work with Professor Kennedy at a hospital in Hartford, Connecticut. Klaus's heart sank when he looked at a map of Connecticut. Hartford and New Haven were forty miles apart. How would they ever see each other if Tina had to commute eighty miles round-trip each day?

In early spring 1991, Klaus and Tina flew to the United States to investigate their new positions. Upon arrival in New Haven, Tina called Professor Kennedy to set up an appointment to see him, only to discover that the professor had moved from Hartford. He was now head of pediatrics at Bridgeport Hospital, which was also a Yale teaching hospital. Professor Kennedy apologized for the switch, and then he made Tina an offer—she could join him at the hospital in Bridge-port if she wanted. Bridgeport and New Haven were just twelve miles apart.

When he heard the news, Klaus stood in their hotel room staring at Tina in amazement. Not only would they be working close to each other, but they would also both be working at Yale teaching hospitals.

Following their visit to Connecticut, Klaus and Tina flew back to England, where they crammed their belongings into their old Talbot Horizon car and headed for Dover and the ferry to France. After two and a half years in Great Britain, it was time to head back to Germany before going to the United States to take up their residencies.

The Germany they returned to was different from the one they had left. On October 3, 1990, following the negotiation of a treaty between East and West Germany, East Germany had ceased to exist as a separate country and had joined the Federal Republic of Germany. For the first time since the end of World War II, Germany was once again united. It was strange for Klaus to return to a country that was no longer divided.

The two hospitals in Connecticut wanted Klaus and Tina to start their residencies in July, which meant they had three months to spare. It did not take them long to decide what they should do with the extra time—another world adventure. This time they would pack their backpacks and head for South America, specifically Peru, Bolivia, and Ecuador.

Klaus and Tina were excited about the trip, but not everyone shared their enthusiasm. This had a lot to do with the "Shining Path," or *Sendero Luminoso*, as it was called in Spanish. Just as they had when they traveled to Ghana, Klaus and Tina were about to step into a volatile political situation. The more Klaus read about Sendero Luminoso and the situation in Peru, the more he understood why people were worried about them. Sendero Luminoso was an insurgent group fighting to destroy the stratified structure of Peruvian society and in its place establish a utopian communist society. The group operated in the Andean highlands of Peru, where they carried out bombings of government buildings and transport networks in the hope of creating a peasant uprising that would spread throughout Peru. For a long time, Sendero Luminoso seemed to have the upper hand in their fight against the Peruvian government. However, Peru's new president, Alberto Fujimori, had redoubled military efforts to rid the country of the group. Klaus was glad to read that the military seemed to be making at least some headway in this effort.

To make matters worse, the German newspapers reported that a cholera epidemic had broken out in Peru. This was on top of the country's economic woes. Inflation had skyrocketed to 7,600 percent under the previous president, and long lines formed outside grocery stores for daily necessities. Klaus was amazed how like Ghana it all sounded. Somehow he and Tina had a knack for visiting countries in the midst of turmoil. Despite this, they were determined to go on their trip, and they plunged into a crash course to learn some basic Spanish. After two weeks of intensive language study, Klaus felt prepared enough to embark on their adventure to South America.

After arriving in Lima, the capital of Peru, Klaus and Tina made their way south along the coast to Arequipa. From there they traveled over the mountains to Lake Titicaca, the largest inland lake in South America and the highest navigable lake in the world. From Puno, on the shore of Lake Titicaca, they took a short flight to La Paz, the capital of Bolivia. After returning to Puno, they took the train northward to Cusco in southeastern Peru.

Klaus had been fascinated by the Inca Empire for as long as he could remember. He was amazed that without a written language the Incas had managed to govern an empire that stretched from Southern Ecuador to northern Chile and included a vast swath of the Amazon basin across the Andes. He was also amazed at how such a great empire had been so easily conquered by a handful of Spanish conquistadors over 450 years before.

In Cusco, Klaus was in the capital of the old Inca Empire. It was truly a wonderful place, filled with Spanish colonial buildings along with remnants of Inca buildings. Klaus marveled at the vastness of the old Inca fortress of Saksaywaman that sat on the hill above the city. He could scarcely believe how intricate the stonework was that formed the fortress's walls. While in Cusco, Klaus and Tina traveled to Machu Picchu to see the Inca ruins. Klaus admired the vastness and the quality of the stonework at this site. He wondered how the Incas had managed to move so many stones up the almost sheer mountain faces on both sides of the ridge upon which Machu Picchu sat, high above the Urubamba River.

In a Cusco bookshop Klaus found a copy of the *Royal Commentaries of the Incas* by Garcilaso de la Vega, the son of a Spanish conquistador and an Inca noblewoman. Born in 1539, de la Vega had written the story of the sixteenth-century Incas. Klaus read the book in just a few days. It was riveting. While he read, Klaus could not help but compare what he was learning with the descendants of the Incas—the Quechua people, who made up half the population of Peru. The Quechuas had such a proud history to look back on, yet as far as Klaus could tell, the people seldom laughed or even smiled. By any standard their lives were grim. Klaus had seen their mud-and-straw houses spread across the countryside with no electricity, running water, sewers, or even glass panes in the windows. A taxi driver had told Klaus that the one point of pride was their language, which they still spoke, using Spanish only as a second language.

As a doctor Klaus was interested in healthcare, and what he saw in the Andes left a lot to be desired. The Quechuas' deplorable living conditions were a breeding ground for all manner of diseases, from tuberculosis to skin infections. A cholera epidemic had taken hold in Peru, with the hospitals ill equipped and in need of doctors. As far as Klaus could see, these doctors needed to be willing to roll up their sleeves and take the initiative in caring for people. The Quechuas needed more than just pills and injections. They hungered for love and respect, but instead were treated like second-class citizens in their own country. It was easy to understand why a terrorist group like Sendero Luminoso, with its goal of overthrowing the government in Lima, would appeal to the people of the mountains of Peru, especially when that government seemed to have forgotten them.

From Peru Klaus and Tina traveled on to Ecuador. By the end of their trip, they were more determined than ever to get all the medical qualifications they needed and head out to the mission field—perhaps in one of the three countries they had just visited.

By the end of July 1991, Klaus and Tina had settled into a rented cottage by the sea in Milford, Connecticut, halfway between New Haven and Bridgeport, and were busy at work in their respective hospitals. To keep their focus on the future, they held "Third World Evenings" in their home. Once a month they invited students and faculty from Yale to gather to listen to a speaker, normally someone they knew who had recently visited a developing country. These meetings encouraged Klaus and Tina to keep alive the dream of serving the poor and alerted many of their new friends to the possibilities of worldwide service.

Not long after Klaus had arrived at the Yale University School of Medicine in New Haven, Dr. C. Elton Cahow, a professor of surgery at the hospital, explained to him how Klaus had come to be selected for the position. "I was on my sabbatical, so I didn't have time to make decisions about new residents. I happened to go into my office one day to pick up some papers, and I saw your application on my desk. I read through it, and since everything seemed in order, I wrote a note offering you the position. Later I got rapped over the knuckles for that. I really should have gone through the admissions board, but I was on sabbatical, and besides, it's working out for you, isn't it?"

Klaus smiled. It sounded very much like the way he'd been accepted into the Medical College of Virginia five years before.

Klaus also described to his supervisor, Professor Irvin Modlin, his dream of being a doctor in the developing world. Professor Modlin was from South Africa, and he had one piece of advice for Klaus: "If you really want to operate a lot, you have to go to South Africa."

"Why's that?" Klaus asked.

"There is nothing like Baragwanath Hospital anywhere else in the world," Professor Modlin replied. "It's the largest hospital in the southern hemisphere—three thousand beds. It serves over four million people who live in the surrounding area. There's terrible civil strife there due to political unrest, but you'll have the opportunity to do hundreds of operations that you hardly see in the First World—gunshot wounds by the dozen, machete slashings, amputations—all day, every day. If you want to get good at surgery fast, South Africa is the place for you."

Klaus had to admit that this sounded like a good next step, and after he and Tina completed their two-year commitments at Yale, they moved to South Africa. They arrived in Johannesburg in July 1993. Even though Klaus thought he knew what they were getting into, he was shocked by what he saw. South Africa was in turmoil. The country had used a system of laws to keep the white and black races separate, with the whites holding almost all the political power and resources. This institutional racism was known in South Africa as apartheid. However, in 1991, under mounting international pressure, the government of South Africa finally repealed apartheid laws and formally recognized black political parties, such as the African National Congress.

When Klaus arrived, the country was on track to hold its first-ever free, multiracial election. But this, in turn, had created political chaos. A state of near anarchy existed in some areas, with many of the nation's civil structures falling apart and violence and crime paralyzing much of daily life. Every month, thousands of cars were hijacked on the street, and drivers were killed in a hail of bullets. To make matters worse, free from the constraints of apartheid, many blacks began engaging in tribal warfare with each other. It was not uncommon to see South Africans, both white and black, armed with weapons.

Despite the political turmoil in the country, Professor Modlin had been right—South Africa was the place to get a lot of surgical experience fast. Klaus found himself thrust into a whirlwind of three hundred patients a day. One after the other, patients were rolled into the operating room with everything from bullet and stab wounds to infected burns and large boils that needed lancing. Klaus would race from amputating a leg to stopping the bleeding and extracting the bullet from the chest of a patient with a gunshot wound.

Tina was experiencing a similar work overload in the pediatrics department. Every month the load increased as qualified staff—nurses, doctors, medical technicians—relocated to just about any country that would accept them. Klaus and Tina found it hard to socialize with other doctors. Everyone had stories to tell about friends who had been kidnapped or murdered during the chaos in the country. Klaus and Tina prayed when coming and going from the hospital, as they felt especially vulnerable out on the road in a car.

Worse than this, Klaus soon discovered that there was little or no compassion for critically injured patients once they were admitted to the hospital. Black South Africans came from two main tribal groups, the Zulu and Xhosa tribes. Much to Klaus's dismay, the staff at the hospital were unable to leave those divisions at the door when they came to work. When a Xhosa man came in with a bullet wound to his head, a critical injury that required close attention from a Zulu nurse, she could hardly be bothered to attend to the man. Klaus watched as she checked her phone messages and made a few personal calls while the patient groaned in agony. Eventually he told the nurse to put down her phone and get on with her job, but the experience shook him to the core. If a nurse would ignore a patient when the doctor was in the same room, what kind of treatment did that patient get when the doctor left?

Another issue both Klaus and Tina had to contend with was AIDS. Like all the other hospital staff, they had to be careful not to accidentally prick themselves with the needles of syringes and possibly contract the AIDS virus. About a third of Tina's young patients had AIDS, and many were orphans who had lost their parents to the disease. Klaus listened as doctors told him stories of how they had gone to villages out in the countryside and found only a couple of old men and a few little children left. Everyone else had died of AIDS. It was a grim reality and a reminder of the tremendous medical challenges that existed in undeveloped countries.

In early 1994 Tina learned she was pregnant. Klaus was excited to think he was going to be a father.

Four months later, in April 1994, following South Africa's first free and multiracial election, the African National Congress was elected to power, with the party's leader, Nelson Mandela, becoming president. Klaus was hopeful that things would begin to settle down in the country.

On September 6, 1994, Tina gave birth to a daughter, whom they named Natalie. Klaus was delighted, but he quickly found that fatherhood changed his thinking about putting himself and Tina into risky situations. Now they had a child to consider. Despite high hopes for peace and stability after the election, South Africa still faced a lot of violence, and many European staff left the country. *Is it time for our family to leave as well?* Klaus wondered. He and Tina had gained much experience at Baragwanath Hospital, yet they both felt their time in South Africa was drawing to a close.

In July 1995 the John family boarded an airplane to return to Germany.

Chapter 7

Was This Where He Was Meant to Be?

Even though Klaus and Tina had not lived in Germany for seven years, they soon slipped back into a routine, this time in Marwitz, a town located on the northern edge of Berlin. Klaus had signed a contract to work at the Virchow Clinic, which was attached to the Berlin University Hospital. He planned to qualify as a surgeon after one year there. While Klaus commuted into Berlin each morning, Tina opted to stay home with baby Natalie.

For Klaus, work at the Virchow Clinic was demanding but interesting. It took him a while to get used to the austere protocol that existed among German medical staff. Nonetheless, under the supervision of senior physicians, he got to carry out laparoscopic gall bladder removals and even removed a cancerous stomach for the first time. The clinic was famous for its expertise in liver transplants, and Klaus also got to participate in a number of these surgeries.

The first year at the Virchow Clinic sped by, and at the end of it Klaus passed his surgeon's exam. Now that he was a qualified surgeon, he felt he was at a crossroad in his career. Professor Peter Neuhaus, head surgeon at the hospital, strongly urged Klaus to continue with his medical education and pursue a professorship. This could take four to six years of grueling study and preparation. That was one option. The other option was to follow his dream of being a doctor in the Third World.

For a brief moment, the offer of becoming a professor was tempting. Klaus thought about all of the positive aspects—wealth, prestige, a great education for his children, living in a modern society, being near his parents in their old age. But how did all these things stack up against his and Tina's call to be missionary doctors? They didn't. Klaus knew he still needed more experience, but his goal was to work in a developing country. He knew he would get there eventually.

August 1996 was a significant month for Klaus. On the third, Tina gave birth to a son, whom they named Dominik. Once again Klaus was a proud father. Later that month Klaus learned of a German missionary doctor named Eckehart Wolff, who worked with the Christian radio station HCJB in Quito, Ecuador.

Klaus decided to write to him for advice. A reply from Dr. Wolff came back in record time. Klaus read it carefully. "We urgently need a surgeon at Hospital Vozandes del Oriente in Shell. The hospital is situated on the edge of the Ecuadorian jungle. Please come. You will be able to perform every operation you have ever learned."

Klaus read the letter again. Where had he heard of a place called Shell before? Then it came to him. Years ago he had read the book *Through Gates of Splendor* by Elisabeth Elliot. The book told the story of Elisabeth's husband, Jim, who, along with Nate Saint (a Mission Aviation Fellowship pilot) and three other young missionary men, was speared to death by an Ecuadorian jungle tribe. Klaus remembered that Nate and his family had lived in Shell.

It was a sobering moment. Germany seemed such a safe place to raise a family compared to the jungles of Ecuador, where one could possibly die at the end of a spear. Still, Klaus could not dismiss the idea of working at a hospital in Ecuador without seeing the place firsthand. He talked it over with Tina, who agreed that he should spend a week in Ecuador to see the country and the hospital for himself. In February 1997 Klaus took a week's vacation from the clinic and flew to Quito.

As the airplane circled to land in Quito, Klaus had a clear view of Mount Pichincha, the active volcano on whose eastern slope Quito was located. In the distance he could see the snow-capped peaks of two other volcanoes, Cotopaxi and Illiniza. Dr. Wolff picked Klaus up at the airport and drove him through the historic old center of the city to his house, where Klaus stayed with the doctor and his wife and family for two days. Dr. Wolff showed Klaus around the hospital that HCJB ran in Quito.

While with the Wolffs, Klaus learned as much as possible about life in Ecuador. Dr. Wolff pointed out that although the equator passed just north of Quito, the city sat in the mountains at an elevation of 9,350 feet and the weather could get quite cool at times. That was not the case in Shell, where Hospital Vozandes del Oriente was located. There, in the Amazon basin, both the climate and the landscape were very different. Klaus saw this clearly for himself as he flew out of Quito in a four-seater Cessna airplane, operated by Mission Aviation Fellowship (MAF), bound for Shell. As they crossed the Andes, the land on the eastern side of the mountains fell away to reveal dense jungle crisscrossed by many rivers.

"This area is known as the Oriente, and all those rivers flow into the Amazon," the pilot noted and then proceeded to name the various rivers for Klaus. "And that volcano in the distance, that's Mount Sangay."

As the Cessna approached Shell, the pilot explained the name. "In the 1930s and 40s, the Shell Oil Company explored for oil in this region, drilling many wells. They built a landing strip and a small town in the jungle to service their efforts, and that place was known as Shell. The company eventually abandoned its search for oil in the Oriente in 1949, leaving behind the airstrip and the town. Nate Saint established MAF's operation in Ecuador here in 1948."

When the door to the Cessna swung open, Klaus was immediately assaulted by the extreme heat and humidity of the rainforest. Dr. Roger Smalligan, an American missionary doctor, was waiting to meet Klaus and show him the hospital. Dr. Smalligan explained that a two-room missionary clinic had opened in Shell in 1955. The clinic was replaced in 1958 by a fourteen-bed hospital that was erected next to the clinic. Nate Saint had been instrumental in seeing the hospital established. He had donated the land and had built much of the hospital himself. Regrettably, he never lived to see it completed.

Over the years other service buildings, such as housing for medical staff and a generator shed to provide electric power, had sprung up around the original hospital. When the original hospital became too small, a new one was opened in 1985 across the Motolo River, with a suspension bridge linking the two hospital sites.

As they walked through Hospital Vozandes del Oriente, which consisted of two long, low wings parallel to each other and connected in the middle, Dr. Smalligan talked about the possibilities.

"We haven't had a permanent surgeon here for six years," the doctor said in his southern drawl. "Visiting surgeons from around the world come to help from time to time, and so the number of surgeries performed at the hospital fluctuates. That's why there is only one surgical patient in the hospital at the moment."

The thought of one lone surgical patient deflated Klaus, who had expected to find a facility pulsing with activity, much like the hospital in South Africa. Instead he was presented with a small, understaffed structure in the middle of the jungle.

Klaus didn't know what to think. Was this small, twenty-five-bed hospital where all his years of medical training and surgery skills could best be put to use? Was this backwoods town in the Amazon basin of Ecuador where he wanted to bring his wife and children to live?

Klaus paced the floor at the Quito airport as he waited for a flight to Bogotá, Colombia, where he would connect with a flight to Paris. He was still unsure about working at Hospital Vozandes del Oriente, and he had made no commitments to return. He walked past a group of passengers huddled by the departure gate at the far end of the room. Soon afterward, a flight attendant came out and talked to the people at the gate. Klaus strolled back to find out what was going on. He spoke to a large man in a crumpled suit. "Did the attendant have any information on the flight?" he asked the man in English.

"Not really. She just told us the plane would be ready soon. I hope it's not too long. After this I still have a long flight from Bogotá to Paris," the man said in a thick German accent.

Klaus thought about saying "Me too," but he was in no mood for a long conversation. He guessed that the man was a German tourist, and he couldn't be bothered with small talk. He walked back to his seat and sat down. The boarding call for the flight was finally made, and Klaus took his cramped seat on the airplane. He tried to ignore the woman beside him, who used the whole armrest between them to file her fingernails.

As the plane took off and made its way north to Bogotá, Klaus thought about what he would tell Tina. He had no idea, really. He wondered whether God even wanted them to go to Shell. How was burying themselves in a tiny jungle hospital going to get them any closer to their goal? There were millions of poor, sick people in the world. Surely there were busier hospitals where his and Tina's medical skills could be utilized.

When the plane landed in Bogotá, Klaus and the other passengers flying on to international destinations were escorted to a large transit lounge. Klaus nodded to a couple of people he recognized from the Quito airport. He then headed to the far corner of the lounge, where he could be left in peace to read and think. He had just settled into a plastic chair when the man from Quito, the one he supposed was a German tourist, plopped himself down in a chair beside Klaus. "Well, we meet again," the man said cheerfully.

Klaus held up the book of short stories he'd just pulled from his bag, trying to send the message that he did not want to enter into conversation.

But the man did not take the hint. "So what brought you to Ecuador? I assume that's where you've been," he asked in German this time.

"Visiting a hospital," Klaus replied brusquely.

"How interesting. I hope you're not sick."

"No," Klaus said. "I'm not."

"Why a hospital then?" the man asked. "Are you a medical rep?"

Klaus took a deep breath. *How come the most annoying man in this huge room has chosen to inflict himself on me? Can't he see I want to be alone?* he thought before replying, "No, I'm a doctor."

"A doctor, how interesting. What hospital did you visit? What did you think of the medical care in Quito?"

Klaus sighed and tucked the book back into his bag. It was obvious the man had no idea about good manners, and there was nothing Klaus could do but talk to him.

"Actually, I've been in the jungle, at Hospital Vozandes del Oriente," Klaus said. "It's operated by missionaries, and my wife, who is a doctor as well, and I are thinking of working there." Then he added, "I'm a surgeon."

"Really?" the man said. "And what church are you a member of?"

Klaus was too tired to get into a theological debate, so he said, "It's a very small denomination in Germany. You've probably never heard of it."

"I might have. What is it called?" the man persisted.

Klaus glared at him. *How could he possibly be so nosy?* Finally, he let out a sigh and said, "It's an Evangelical Free Church."

"You don't say! I belong to an Evangelical Free Church in Essen," the man replied gleefully.

There was a long pause. Klaus felt a little embarrassed that he had been so unfriendly toward a fellow Christian, but the man did not seem to be bothered by it.

"This is a turn of events," the man said, thrusting out his hand. "My name's Wolfgang Hasselhuhn."

"Klaus John," Klaus said, shaking the man's hand.

Wolfgang continued. "My wife died of lung cancer four weeks ago, and I was in a deep, dark hole. My brother is an aid worker in Ecuador, and he invited me to visit him, so that's why I've been here. It's been good to get out and see something different."

Klaus did not know what to say.

Wolfgang's face brightened. "Well, I've just had a wonderful thought. I head up our church's outreach program to developing nations. Maybe we could support your work in Ecuador."

Suddenly a wave of faith engulfed Klaus. He could see the future. God had arranged for him and Wolfgang Hasselhuhn to meet. Wolfgang and his church would be their first supporters as the John family moved to Shell to work at the hospital. Unexplainably, Klaus knew beyond a doubt that he was on the right track after all. He could hardly wait to get home and tell Tina what had happened.

Back in Berlin, Klaus eagerly told Tina about meeting Wolfgang Hasselhuhn. Tina was as excited about it as he was. However, things did not go so smoothly back at Virchow Clinic when Klaus announced that he was planning to move to Ecuador. Professor Neuhaus was personally insulted that Klaus would throw away the opportunity to continue studying under him. He took Klaus off the surgery roster and told him that he would not be reassigned to operate unless he changed his mind. Instead, Klaus was placed on duty in the intensive care unit, far from the drama of the operating room. Klaus was disappointed, but he was too excited about the future to let it bother him much.

In the summer of 1997 Klaus completed his contract at Virchow Clinic. True to his word, Professor Neuhaus had not allowed him to do a single surgery since he arrived back from Ecuador.

Now that they had a destination in mind, Klaus and Tina made plans for their future. They agreed that Klaus should spend the next year at home, looking after the children during the day and making preparations for Ecuador at night, while Tina went back to the hospital to complete her pediatric residency. Then, if all went well, they would head for Ecuador at the end of summer 1998.

On January 1, 1998, Klaus sat down to write the John family's first-ever missionary newsletter. He called it *Die Johns Ärzte Für Indios* (The Johns, Medical Doctors for the Indians). He typed away:

> By presenting our slide show all over the country, we are getting to know Germany quite well. The cities of Oranienburg, Essen, Dortmund, Weimar, Dusseldorf, Wiesbaden, Alzey, Bremen, and Berlin are just a few

stopovers on our journey across the republic. We traveled on the German highways for
thousand of miles and had to load and unload
our car countless times. . . . The countdown
has begun, and the day of our departure is
approaching.

Klaus went on to explain that they had signed up
with the VDM (United German Missionary Aid), a
German-based organization that helped missionaries
from many denominations complete the necessary
paperwork, find the right insurance, and administer
their money while they were overseas. After talking
to many people, Klaus and Tina set a goal of raising
$5,000 a month for their support. This amount would
cover their living expenses, travel, insurance, and
taxes, and would allow them to pay into their retire-
ment funds. Klaus wrote in the first newsletter that
the people they had met while speaking in churches,
civic meetings, and small private gatherings around
Germany had pledged a total of $1,500 toward their
goal so far. They were 30 percent of the way there.
Some of that amount came from the Evangelical Free
Church in Essen, just as Wolfgang Hasselhuhn had
suggested it would.

The months flew by. At night Klaus learned Spanish and took a Bible correspondence course, all to
better equip himself for the work ahead. In July 1998
Tina passed her Pediatric Board exams. Everything
was on track. The family moved out of their row
house in Marwitz and back to Wiesbaden to live with
Klaus's parents as they made final preparations to

leave Germany. Klaus continued to pray and work hard at raising their monthly support, but they were still short of their monthly support goal by $1,800.

Just as it had been when they were preparing to go to Ghana and South Africa, news of Ecuador seemed to fill the newspapers. Most of what was reported was not good: inflation was sky high in the country; an El Niño had caused disastrous flooding along the coast; the price of gasoline, electricity, and transportation was exorbitant; and a Tupolev airplane operated by Cubana Airlines had crashed on takeoff from Quito on August 29, 1998, killing seventy of the ninety-one passengers and crew aboard and another ten people on the ground. Despite the grim headlines, Klaus and Tina were not deterred from the path they had chosen.

On September 6, 1998, the day before the John family was to fly out of Germany for Ecuador, Klaus sat down and updated the financial spreadsheet on his computer. He used it to keep track of the monthly pledges that had been made toward their support. He entered the last two pledges and pressed the return key. The total at the bottom of the spreadsheet was exactly $5,000. Klaus sat in shock and awe. He and Tina had prayed for $5,000 in monthly support, they had worked hard to raise the amount, and now there it was in front of him—not one cent over or one cent under.

Chapter 8

Surgeon-in-Chief

On May 10, 1999, Klaus walked through the doors of Hospital Vozandes del Oriente. Six months of Spanish language study in Quito were behind him, and it was time to begin the life he had planned and worked toward for so long. At thirty-eight years of age he was officially Dr. Klaus-Dieter John, Surgeon-in-Chief. The thought sobered him. It had been a little over two years since Professor Neuhaus had taken him off the operating roster at Virchow Clinic, and he hadn't performed surgery since that time. He looked at his hands and hoped he still remembered how to use the surgical instruments with skill and precision.

Klaus's skills were soon tested when Andri Naichap, a pretty little girl from the jungle, arrived at the hospital. A venomous snake had bitten Andri on the heel of her foot seven weeks before. A serious infection had developed, and Andri's relatives had taken her to the local witch doctor for treatment, which Klaus soon learned was a common practice in the jungle. Without proper medicine and treatment for the bite, Andri's condition deteriorated quickly. Eventually she was flown to Shell and brought to the hospital, where it was expected that her leg would have to be amputated.

Klaus knew that the amputation would leave Andri with a bleak outlook. She would never have the chance to marry and would need to be carried everywhere. Without a leg, Andri's life in the jungle would be one of loneliness and ridicule. Even though it would be difficult, Klaus decided to try to save her leg. He began a series of operations to cut away all the dead and infected tissue on her foot and leg until he was satisfied he had gotten it all. Every day the nurses changed the dressings and treated Andri's wounds with antibiotics. After seven operations, Klaus won the battle: Andri's leg was saved. Once the infection was gone, Klaus was able to close the wounds with a skin graft.

One evening Klaus was about to walk home to the house he and Tina had rented in Shell when he heard a commotion in the hospital driveway. He rushed outside to see what it was. "Hurry! Hurry! Can someone here help us?" he heard a man yell.

Klaus quickly sized up the situation. Four cars were parked in front of the hospital with their doors open. Several men were carefully pulling people from the backseat of two of the cars. By now two nurses were running toward the cars with stretchers.

"What happened?" Klaus asked in Spanish.

"A motorbike accident. There's no surgeon at the hospital at Puyo—it's carnival time and everyone is out partying—so they sent us here. They said we need a surgeon," one of the men said. "Are you a surgeon?"

Klaus nodded as he watched two people—a young man and a young woman—being lifted gently onto stretchers. Klaus took a deep breath and said a prayer for guidance and strength. Then he hurried through the hospital doors. It would be many hours before he returned home.

Inside he learned that the motorcycle the young man and woman were riding had run head-on into a truck. Both riders had suffered multiple, serious fractures and lacerations. Klaus went straight to work setting broken bones and stitching up cuts. He shook his head as he thought about the first hospital where the pair had sought help and how no one was available to attend to them because all the doctors were out partying. That would be unthinkable in Germany. Hadn't they heard of the concept of one doctor being on call at all times?

Meanwhile, as Klaus kept busy as chief surgeon, Tina began working three days a week in the pediatrics ward. She also made house calls on sick children in town. Then in August the Johns received the good news that Tina was again pregnant. Even so, Tina was determined to keep up her work at the hospital.

Early in his time at Hospital Vozandes del Oriente, Klaus was relieved when an Australian surgeon, Michael Stathis, arrived to volunteer for two
months. Dr. Stathis, who was sixty years old, proved
to be a big help. He had volunteered at many mission
hospitals around the world, and Klaus was grateful
to have such a knowledgeable mentor.

One Tuesday morning, Klaus and Dr. Stathis were
in the operating room together, removing an elderly
woman's thyroid gland, when Dr. Steve Manock, one
of the hospital's general practitioners, burst in. "Klaus!
Michael! You have to do an emergency C-section
now!" he said.

"We can't," Klaus replied. "This is the trickiest
part of the operation. Send the woman to Puyo. This
will take us another hour."

"We don't have time!" Steve insisted. "If we don't
do a C-section right now—right this minute—the
baby will die, and probably the mother too."

"Okay," Klaus said, thinking fast. They had one
anesthesiologist and two surgeons. "Steve, you take
over watching this anesthesia machine. Dr. Stathis,
can you manage here?"

Michael nodded.

"Then I guess I'm doing a C-section," Klaus said
as he put down his scissors and ran out of the operating room. A minute later he was in a clean gown,
standing beside a woman gasping in pain. The
anesthesiologist, who had followed Klaus from the
other operating room, was already administering
anesthesia.

Klaus swabbed the woman's belly as the anesthetic began to take effect. Inside was a baby, and he was about to cut through skin, tissue, and muscle to get it out. Despite all the surgeries Klaus had performed in his life, he had never before performed a C-section. He had no time before starting to read up on the finer details of the operation from his surgical textbooks.

Klaus prayed for God to guide him and picked up the scalpel. His pulse raced as he made a firm incision into the abdominal wall. Now was not the time to be hesitant. The fetal heart monitor showed the baby's heart rate dipping very low. Klaus worked fast. He put his hand into the incision and felt for the baby. There it was! He grasped the head and body and carefully lifted the baby out. An infant's cry filled the room. Klaus placed the child—a little girl—beside her mother and cut the umbilical cord.

As he sutured the mother's abdomen, Klaus was filled with gratitude—gratitude that everything had gone well and that he had been able to save two lives, and gratitude that after twenty years of training he was finally doing what he had worked so long and hard to achieve.

Klaus had expected as a missionary doctor to share his faith with others, but sometimes he found that his patients lifted his own faith with their remarkable stories. One of these people was a man named Humberto Tangamash. Humberto had fallen out of a tree as a young man and shattered his spine. He was paraplegic and was admitted to the hospital with a raging infection in his buttocks. The surgery to deal with the infection left Humberto in pain for many days as he recuperated. Despite the pain, Humberto used his time at the hospital to work on a personal project—translating the Bible into his Shuar language. Whenever Klaus visited Humberto to check on his recovery, Humberto was always smiling and ready to discuss his translation work.

Another patient who lifted Klaus's faith was Claudia, a Waorani Indian. He came to the hospital for surgery, and Klaus asked to pray with him beforehand. Claudia confessed that forty-five years before, his uncle had taken part in the murder of the five missionaries along the Curaray River. Thankfully, the murders had not stopped the gospel from eventually coming to his tribe.

"It changed us," Claudia told Klaus. "We were violent, and we killed for revenge. But now we do not. I would probably not have lived beyond twenty back then. There were few old people in the tribe. Most died in the revenge killings. But now I am thirty-six years old. The Christian message changed our tribe from the inside out."

Klaus was deeply touched by Claudia's comments. It was good to hear firsthand that the gospel was bringing real change to the lives of people in the jungles of the Oriente. Klaus was glad to be a link in that chain.

While on a trip to Quito, Klaus learned of a problem the HCJB-run hospital there was having with getting its new radiography equipment through customs. The container with the equipment had been shipped from Miami to the port of Guayaquil. However, before it was sealed for shipment in Miami, someone had thrown a bag of used clothes into the container. Klaus supposed some well-meaning person probably thought the clothes could be used for poor patients. But now that bag of clothes was causing all kinds of problems. Because the bag was not listed on the cargo manifest, customs officers had refused to release the container, saying it needed to be shipped back to Miami to have the manifest document amended and then returned to Guayaquil.

The situation seemed ludicrous to Klaus. Why didn't customs just throw the bag of clothes away and pass the equipment that was listed on the manifest? Why would they want the whole container sent back to the United States over a bag of clothes? Didn't they know the new radiography equipment would help save lives? And who was to say that if the container had been shipped back to Miami and then returned to Guayaquil that customs wouldn't have found some other issue with it—a stamp that was not on a form, or some piece of paper that was not duplicated properly?

Deep down Klaus knew the root the problem: the whole legal system in Ecuador, from issuing a traffic ticket to importing life-saving equipment through customs, had one thing in common—bribery. Klaus had experienced this firsthand. He had been attempting to pay his car tax for some time now. In Germany this would have taken half an hour to complete, but not in Ecuador. So far he'd visited fourteen different authorities and made six trips to the bank, and still the issue was not resolved. Apparently some clerk had checked the wrong box on a form the year before. Several officials had suggested that a "donation" would make the problem go away, but Klaus was determined to see the situation rectified without paying a bribe.

In Guayaquil, customs officers were already hinting that a large amount of money dropped into the right hands would solve the problem with the container. But as a Christian organization, Radio HCJB had a policy of never paying bribes. But neither did the organization have the money to pay for the container to be shipped back to the United States and then returned to Ecuador. So the situation with the container was at a stalemate.

On a subsequent trip to Quito, Klaus learned the fate of the container and the new radiography equipment it contained. The stalemate had dragged on until the container accrued so many fines and storage fees that HCJB made the decision to let it go. Customs officers seized the radiography equipment, and no one in customs seemed to know what happened to it after that.

When he got back to Shell, Klaus told Tina about the situation with the container. It bothered her as much as it did Klaus. They both wondered what could have been done to prevent losing the radiography equipment. As far as Klaus could see, the best protection against paying bribes was having friends in high places.

"Look, Tina," he said. "If an organization has a patron, someone like the Minister of Health, government officials wouldn't dare confiscate its stuff or mess with it."

Tina agreed. "That's just another thing we'll have to contend with, isn't it? We must remember this lesson."

Klaus nodded. Tina was talking about their dream—a dream that had been forming over years and about which they had not yet told anyone else. It was a dream that one day the two of them would build their own hospital somewhere in South America to serve the very poorest people.

The time working at the hospital in Shell was teaching Klaus and Tina many important lessons they hoped would help them make their dream a reality. The first lesson, the one they had just learned, was that foreigners working in South America needed strong links with powerful people in the country they were serving so that they could work without paying bribes.

Another lesson they were learning was that any hospital whose purpose was to reach the poorest people had to be funded from outside the country. It cost about $50,000 a month to run Hospital Vozandes del Oriente, an amount that covered the cost of salaries for their fifty Ecuadorian employees as well as drugs, maintenance, and materials. It was a heavy financial burden each month, and Radio HCJB had changed its policy toward the institution. It declared that Hospital Vozandes del Oriente had to become self-sufficient, meaning the actual costs of running the hospital had to be met by the patients it treated.

Although the hospital always said that it was there to serve all people, Klaus noticed a change begin to take place with this new policy—more middle-class people were admitted for treatment, and often poor people, who could not pay, were turned away. A number of the hospital staff, including Klaus and Tina, gave toward a charity fund to help cover the cost of treatment of these poor patients, but it was never enough. Klaus hoped to avoid this situation in "their" new hospital by getting adequate funding from Western countries, ensuring that everyone who needed care would get it.

At 5:10 on the afternoon of April 11, 2000, in the hospital, Tina gave birth to another son, whom she and Klaus named Florian. The Johns now had three children, each born on a different continent: Natalie in Africa, Dominik in Europe, and now Florian in South America. Klaus joked that it was going to be quite a job updating their passports.

When Florian was five months old, Klaus set off on an explorative visit to Peru and Bolivia. He hoped to find a place to build a mission hospital, or at least that is what he told other people. However, as Klaus flew over the Andes from Shell to Quito, he found himself asking more and more questions. The idea of building a hospital—a big, modern hospital—began to seem like make-believe. Klaus thought about all the steps such a venture would involve—all the equipment, all the money, all the people—and he began to wonder whether he'd been crazy to think he could ever undertake such a task.

In Quito, Klaus stayed in an HCJB guesthouse for a week while he attended to hospital business before departing for Peru and Bolivia. But the extra time in Quito made matters worse for him. His mood grew darker as he wrestled with the idea of building his own hospital.

"Who do I think I'm kidding?" Klaus asked himself aloud. "A hospital like that would cost millions of dollars to build. Imagine all the corruption we would have to overcome, the staff we would have to attract, the contracts and the money it would take to keep it running all year long, year after year. Tina and I are delusional to think such a thing is possible. I should just go back to Shell now and save the money on this trip."

Klaus stared at the blank white wall of the guestroom for a long while before reaching over and picking up his daily devotional journal. He opened to the day's date and began to read from Psalm 32. He read on until he came to verse 8: "I will instruct you and teach you in the way you should go; I will counsel you and watch over you." To Klaus it was as if the verse were written in neon colors. *Yes,* he thought, *that's it. If God says He will instruct me step-by-step, lead me to the right people, open the right doors, then anything is possible! Of course we can build a hospital with God's help. Without it we will surely fail.*

As Klaus put down the devotional journal, he knew something deep inside him had changed. He now had the rock-solid conviction that this mission hospital not only could be built but also *would* be built. It was God's hospital, and God would make it happen. It was the exact same feeling Klaus had had when he talked to Wolfgang Hasselhuhn at the airport in Bogotá three years before. Klaus was certain that something much larger than what his own abilities could create was about to come forth. Now he felt completely different about his fact-finding trip to Peru and Bolivia. He prayed and waited for God to show him the people who could help him make his way through the maze of obstacles he was about to face.

Klaus's first stop on his fact-finding trip was Cochabamba, Bolivia, where Dr. José Miguel de Angulo, a Colombian Christian, ran a small medical station. Regretfully, the visit turned out to be somewhat negative for Klaus. As Klaus explained his long-term goal of building a mission hospital, Dr. de Angulo was bluntly critical of the plan, pointing out that a series of small community clinics like his own was much more realistic. And didn't Klaus know that running such a hospital, let alone building it, was a huge undertaking for just one man?

Undeterred, Klaus flew from La Paz, Bolivia, to Cusco, Peru. As the airplane taxied to the gate, Klaus thought about the first time he'd visited the place with Tina nine and a half years before. It had been an eye-opening experience for Klaus as he had noted the poor state of health care in the region and observed the plight of the Quechua people.

Klaus had come to Cusco to meet with an English missionary doctor named Nat Davis, who had served in Peru for thirty years. Dr. Davis had a totally different attitude from that of Dr. de Angulo in Bolivia. As Klaus described his vision of a hospital to serve the poorest people, Dr. Davis nodded and smiled. "It can be done," he said. "If God wants it to happen, it will happen. I believe He can use you and your wife to build such a hospital. Tell me what I can do to help you."

At that moment Klaus was not quite sure what needed to be done, but he told Nat that he would like to bring Tina and the children to meet him so they could all pray and strategize together.

Three months later, the entire John family was sitting in Dr. Davis's living room in Peru. Natalie and Dominik played with a box of Legos while Florian bounced on Tina's knee. Dr. Davis stated his ideas about what a hospital in Peru or Bolivia would need. Klaus and Tina asked many questions, and as Klaus scribbled pages of notes, he smiled to himself. If an outsider were listening to their conversation, it would sound as though they had all the money in the bank and all the personnel ready to start tomorrow. In fact, they had nothing but a dream and faith that sometime soon a hospital would rise in either Peru or Bolivia.

After their return to Shell, Klaus was determined to keep working on plans for a hospital. Soon, however, other things vied for his attention. He had more surgical cases to take care of: A seventy-three-year-old woman had fallen out of a tree while trying to pick some fruit and had fractured her leg. A thirty-nine-year-old Shuar man had returned from a hunting trip and had leaned on his gun, which discharged thirty pellets into his wrist. A Quechua man who had intended to throw dynamite into the river to catch fish had blown four fingers off his right hand when the powder ignited too soon. Klaus operated on all these patients and soon celebrated the thousandth case he had operated on since arriving at the hospital. He thanked God that not one of those patients had died of complications from surgery. Even in the most modern hospital in Germany, that would have been a great record, and Klaus was certain his prayers before each surgery had made all the difference.

In summer 2001, the John family took their first furlough back home to Germany. They had been away for nearly three years and looked forward to seeing their family and friends. But the trip was also a working vacation. Klaus and Tina had supporters to visit and presentations to give about their work in Shell. During the summer they traveled all over Germany and showed over three thousand people their slides of Ecuador. It was exhausting work with three young children in tow, but Klaus knew it was essential to keep in touch with the Christians who prayed for them and regularly gave money for their monthly support.

As Klaus and Tina traveled, many people asked them about their future plans. Did they intend to stay at the hospital in Shell for years to come? Did they have some other plans? Klaus did not know how to answer their questions. He still believed that God wanted him to build a hospital, but it seemed like such a huge project. And if he had been totally honest with people, he would have told them that he was afraid to start.

Chapter 9

Now or Never

Back in Ecuador on January 18, 2002, the John family was preparing to take a day trip into the mountains from Shell. Klaus called Steve Manock, one of the other doctors, for ideas on the best road to take. Steve had some great suggestions, but before he hung up he said, "By the way, I just found out that our colleague, Jane Weaver, is having difficulty getting her permit to serve as a missionary doctor in Quito. What do you think about having her come to Shell for a year?"

Klaus felt his heart race. Jane was a young American surgeon who would want to share the operating room with him. If Jane came to Shell, it would cut his workload from six hundred surgeries to three hundred a year. The thought did not make Klaus happy—he loved being busy.

Putting his hand over the mouthpiece, Klaus whispered to Tina, "They want Jane Weaver to come here and help me with surgeries. I don't want any help. I'm doing fine."

Tina looked stern. "Klaus," she whispered, "we want to build a hospital. You will need time. Let Jane come."

Klaus stared at Tina for a moment. He knew she was right. If they were to build a hospital, it would take a lot of time. "Sure, send Jane along. She can do all the operations she wants," Klaus told Steve.

When Klaus put down the receiver, Tina said, "Look, we are both over forty. Either we tackle this project now, or it will be too late."

Something deep inside Klaus kicked into action. He knew his wife was right—it was now or never.

The next morning Klaus awoke an hour earlier than normal and went to his desk. With a burst of determination he started writing a proposal for a hospital to be built in either Peru or Bolivia. In the proposal he laid out the reasons for building a new hospital to serve the very poor in the Andes region, a place where the Quechua people would be treated with love and respect and offered the most advanced medical care available. Klaus wrote,

A project such as a medical clinic cannot be devised from scratch overnight. We are aware that the planning and preliminary work may stretch over years. Many people will be alongside us to advise and inspire so that the final product will be a team result. In all our planning, it is our utmost desire to seek God's blessing and guidance in prayer.

As the weeks rolled by, Klaus used every free minute in the evenings and on weekends to hone the proposal. He bought books about Peru and Bolivia and underlined relevant points in them in pencil. He carefully studied maps of both countries and questioned anyone he met who had been to either nation.

Klaus was also excited to discover an old floor plan of the hospital at Shell in a dusty corner. He meticulously copied the plan onto his computer. When he was done, he discussed the layout with Tina and the other doctors and nurses at the hospital. He asked them if there was anything they thought could have been done better or any modern improvements that could be made.

As Klaus spent hours at his desk working on the proposal, the new hospital began to come alive in his head. He could see himself walking through the rooms—the operating room, the intensive care unit, the dental clinic, the large auditorium with stained-glass windows—and he could almost touch the CAT scanner and the oxygen generator that would produce oxygen to flow to patients through wall vents. In the waiting room he imagined hundreds of poor Quechuas waiting to receive the best medical care available. It was all there. He could see it so clearly.

Despite the fact that Jane Weaver did not end up coming to Shell to relieve Klaus's workload, six months after starting on the proposal Klaus had completed the initial draft. The document was fifty pages long and outlined possible locations for the hospital, along with financial and management details. Klaus had even included a sketch of how he saw the finished hospital looking. He estimated that the cost to build the structure would be between one million and three million dollars and would require between twenty-five and thirty skilled volunteers to staff it. The proposal also called for the creation of support organizations in both Germany and South America. Tina carefully read each page of the proposal, making her own additions that were incorporated into the document.

In summer 2002, Klaus knew it was time to make their dream public. He made twenty copies of the proposal and sent them to friends and acquaintances. He asked if they would be willing to join him in setting up an organization to support the hospital, which by now had a name—*Diospi Suyana*, which in the Quechua language means "We trust in God."

The immediate letters and phone calls Klaus and Tina received in response to the proposal were less than enthusiastic. Klaus could sense that many of their supporters thought they had lost touch with reality while living on the edge of the Amazon jungle. So in July 2002 the Johns returned to Germany. They did not tell many people they were coming, since this was not a support-raising trip. It was something much more important—a trip to find out who was on their team.

Back in Germany, Klaus and Tina stayed with Klaus's parents, who were now seventy-seven years old. Klaus's sister Helga did not hold back from telling him what she thought of the idea. "I admire your faith," she said. "But Klaus, you have to be practical. This is a terrible time to ask for support from the people of Germany. Look around you. Things have changed. We are in a bad recession. Unemployment is high. People don't have spare money anymore."

Other people tried to be more positive. One of Klaus's good friends in Berlin told him that it was a great idea but too ambitious. "Why don't you start with a medical clinic for these people? If that goes well, maybe Christians here will be willing to support you in adding a few hospital beds. There's no need to start big. Build up to it. After all, building the hospital won't be the main expense involved, even though that will cost millions. Keeping the place going will be the big cost. How will you ever staff the place and pay all the bills to keep it up and running?"

Another person was worried about Klaus and Tina's accepting anyone's money for such a foolhardy scheme. "Of course, this will be a flop," the person said. "Then what will happen? Do you have any way to pay back the people who will give you money?"

Klaus and Tina listened to everyone's opinion, but they stuck to their plan. They had come to Germany to start a support organization. Now they needed to find the people who believed it was possible to accomplish their goal.

As Klaus prayed about the situation, Olaf Böttger came to mind. Klaus hadn't seen Olaf for over twenty years, but he remembered him as one of the most competent, conscientious, and organized members of the youth group back in the 1970s. Klaus made a few phone calls and was eventually able to track Olaf down. After the two of them caught up on each other's lives, Klaus asked his old friend if he would be willing to serve as the chairperson of the Diospi Suyana organization in Germany.

There was a long pause on the other end of the telephone. "I won't say no," Olaf finally replied. "I'll talk to my wife, Kathrin, about it and get back to you."

Klaus was content with the answer. He knew he was asking a lot of Olaf, but he was sure God would draw the right people to join his team.

On August 17, 2002, eight people joined Klaus and Tina at a hotel in the winter sports resort town of Tabarz in Thuringia. Olaf was there along with his wife, and so was Klaus and Tina's friend Gisela Graf from Wiesbaden with her husband, Ulrich. Klaus was delighted by the turnout. He already knew that under German law, forming a nonprofit organization required a minimum of seven people being present at the constituting sessions—and they had ten.

Klaus and Tina received another encouraging update. After talking with his wife and praying about the matter, Olaf announced that he was willing to take on the position as chairperson. Over the next two days, the group talked and prayed about every aspect of the project. They encouraged each other, and the longer the group was together, the more realistic a three-million-dollar hospital in the Andes felt to Klaus. By the time the meetings drew to a close, the group had composed and refined the necessary statutes for the new nonprofit organization.

Klaus and Tina returned to Ecuador, content they had done what they had set out to do. Now it was time to decide where the hospital should be located. Klaus had pored over maps of South America and come to the conclusion that Abancay Province of the Apurímac region in Peru would be a perfect spot. Abancay was at the junction of two important Peruvian roads: the Caminos del Inca Road, which dated back to Inca times and connected the cities of Nazca and Cusco, and the Via de los Libertadores, which connected the city of Ayacucho to Cusco. This road also formed part of the Pan-American Highway. The province was wracked by extreme poverty. World Health Organization statistics showed fewer than three doctors for every ten thousand people in the region. This was a sober contrast to Germany, where there were thirty-six doctors per ten thousand people.

Apollo Landa was a Peruvian doctor working for a Christian organization in Quito. Klaus and Tina visited Dr. Landa one afternoon, and Klaus asked him where he thought a new hospital should be built in the Andes. Dr. Landa thought for a moment and then said, "The province of Abancay in Peru would be the right area for a hospital, I think."

Klaus felt goose bumps rising on his arms, and he looked at Tina in amazement. Every morning since he started planning the hospital he had read Psalm 32 and asked God to direct his steps. Now, without saying a thing, Apollo Landa had suggested the same area of Peru that Klaus had identified as the possible hospital site. Not only that, but Dr. Landa also promised to do what he could to arrange a meeting for Klaus with the directors of the Evangelical Church Council in both La Paz, Bolivia, and Lima, Peru.

Even more good news followed. One of the missionaries at HCJB suggested that Klaus and Tina meet with Dr. Martin Ruppenthal, the director of the Christian Blind Mission. Dr. Ruppenthal was responsible for 120 projects related to the blind across South America. He proved just as helpful as Apollo Landa, offering to organize meetings for Klaus with the ministers of health in both countries. Klaus was astonished. He had no idea how these two men in Quito were able to open these important doors for him, but he planned to meet with the various officials as soon as meetings could be arranged.

In mid-January 2003, Klaus and a visiting Swiss missionary, Markus Rolli, flew to Bolivia to meet with government representatives and church leaders. Whenever and wherever Klaus presented the idea of a mission hospital, he and Markus received an enthusiastic reception.

From Bolivia, Klaus and Markus flew on to Peru, and on January 23 they boarded a bus in Cusco for the hundred-mile trip along the Pan-American Highway to Abancay. Fields of white anise stretched over the mountain slopes, which were dotted with tiny adobe houses. The highway ran right through the

Apurímac region, known as the poorhouse of Peru. As he peered out the bus window, Klaus could see why. Tiny mud huts with no electricity or window glass were scattered on the hillsides. Groups of women and children gathered at the roadside, where water ran along in the gutters, and washed their babies and plastic plates. The people were small and weathered, and most of the time they didn't even glance up as the bus rolled by.

As the rickety old bus zigzagged up and down the sides of mountains, Klaus prayed they would arrive safely. Bus accidents were a major cause of death in South America. Every time Klaus rode one, he was reminded of the two accidents that had occurred near Shell the year before. In the first accident nine passengers were severely injured, and in the second a bus plunged 750 feet down the side of a mountain, killing thirty-five people. On this day Klaus and Markus arrived safely in the town of Abancay, capital of Abancay Province.

That night Klaus could barely sleep. Loud music was blaring from a radio outside their cheap hotel room, but that wasn't the real problem. Klaus knew it was time to make a decision about the location of the hospital, and he still did not have a clear idea of what to do. He knew it would be pointless going back to Ecuador without a location to report to Tina and the team in Germany, but just where did God want them to be? Klaus agonized over the right decision as he tossed and turned all night.

The following morning Dr. Allen George arrived at the hotel to pick up Klaus and Markus in his 4x4 Jeep. Dr. George and his wife, Amy, were American missionaries who for several years had been working in the mountain areas of Peru. Dr. George had read Klaus's proposal for the hospital and offered to help advise him in finding a suitable location. "We're off to San Luis first," Allen said cheerfully. "It's pretty cold up there, ten thousand feet above sea level, but the village chief is eager to meet you."

When they arrived on the outskirts of San Luis, several hundred people were gathered on a hillside. They wore the brightly colored clothes of the rural Quechua. The chief welcomed the visitors, and Klaus was asked to describe his vision for a hospital. Everyone sat down on the ground as Klaus spoke in Spanish and a local pastor translated into Quechua. The setting was breathtaking, with snowcapped mountains in the background and a patchwork of farms dotting the hills around them. However, as he spoke, Klaus wished he'd packed his jacket. The icy wind whipped through his clothes and chilled him to the bone. As he waited for the interpreter to finish translating his words, he thought about how this was January—the warmest month of the year in the southern hemisphere. Klaus shivered. If this was a summer's day in San Luis, what would a winter's day be like? How would they keep a hospital warm enough up here for the patients?

After Klaus had given his presentation, the chief invited the three visitors to eat dinner with him. As

Klaus ate the guinea pig (*cuy*) and potato soup that were placed in front of him, he knew in his heart that this was not the right location for a hospital.

Following the meal, the three men climbed back into Dr. George's 4x4 and moved on. This time they headed up the Pan-American Highway they had driven down in the bus the day before. To the left was a series of rolling hills, and behind them was a ridge of snowcapped peaks.

"The Apurímac River runs between the hills and the mountains," Allen explained. "It forms a deep canyon where they do a lot of white-water rafting. The mountains are called the Salcantay Range, and Capitan Rumi is the mountain you can see to our left. The Quechuas used to believe—and many still do—that each mountain has a god, or Apu. Apurímac means 'God speaks,' and this valley—the Curahuasi Valley—means 'the house of healing.'"

Klaus watched out the window as they wound down into the valley through fields white with anise. With each turn in the road the air got warmer, until it felt like a spring day in Germany.

"I'm taking you to the town of Curahuasi," Allen said. "I think it might be just what you're looking for."

Soon afterward the 4x4 stopped in front of an adobe brick building with brightly painted blue plaster. A Red Cross sign hung above the door. Klaus laughed. "Driving through here yesterday, I saw another Red Cross sign by the road and thought it meant there was already a hospital here. Now I see it just indicates a clinic. That's good. We don't need to have two hospitals in one town."

"Absolutely not," Dr. George said. "There are so few doctors here and so many needs. Just within three hours' traveling distance of this location are over three quarters of a million people—just about all of them in abject poverty."

The three men stepped into the crumbling medical clinic, which was ill-equipped and offered only the most basic medical care. Yet as he stood in the clinic, Klaus was overcome by an absolute certainty that this place—Curahuasi—was the place for the new hospital. Not far from the Apurímac River, in a beautiful valley, Klaus had found what he had been looking and praying for.

"I'm sure this is the place," Klaus said. "Let's find the mayor."

Allen chuckled. "I thought you might like this valley. Follow me. I know where his office is."

The three men walked up the uneven concrete road toward the town square. Behind the square stood a Catholic church, and beside the square was the town hall. Inside they soon located Julio Cesar Luna, the town's young and energetic mayor. Klaus shook hands with the mayor and came to the point. "We would like to build a hospital here in your valley," he declared.

Mayor Luna looked stunned. "A hospital? Who are you?" he asked.

Klaus showed the mayor a fifteen-page summary of the Diospi Suyana project proposal and explained who he was. It took several minutes for the mayor to grasp the size of the hospital. "Here?" he kept saying. "You want to build this hospital here, in Curahuasi?"

Klaus smiled. He knew how odd it must seem to have three strangers show up at your office and announce that they wanted to change the town forever.

"Just think of that," the mayor said. "The employment opportunities; the ability to get surgery right here. People will come from miles around . . ."

"That's right," Allen said, and then he asked the mayor, "I take it we have your support."

"Of course!" Señor Luna said, a broad smile spreading over his face. "I will do whatever I can to help. When will you start?"

"We are not sure yet," Klaus said. "First we need the right plot of land. Our hope is that it won't be long."

On January 29, 2003, Klaus and Markus Rolli met with the president, the director, and the treasurer of the Evangelical Church Council of Peru in Lima. That was followed on February 3 by a meeting with the Peruvian minister of health, Dr. Carpone Campoverde. As they talked, everyone agreed that Curahuasi was an excellent choice for the site of a new hospital.

Klaus returned to Shell pleased with the progress that had been made. He knew it was just the beginning of a very long road, but at least now he was settled on the direction in which they would be traveling.

Chapter 10

A Place to Build

Back at the hospital in Shell, Klaus continued his work as surgeon while preparing to move to Peru. In addition to the usual surgeries, he had come back to two challenging cases. An eight-year-old girl named Dayana arrived at Hospital Vozandes del Oriente with a sore stomach. Klaus concluded that her condition was serious enough for him to operate. After he had made an incision in Dayana's abdomen, the girl's stomach smelled so bad it was hard for him to keep going.

Klaus soon discovered what the problem was: Dayana's abdominal cavity was filled with pus. Dayana had typhoid fever. Klaus cleaned out the cavity and sutured the incision. During the operation, Dayana's blood pressure dropped so low that the anesthesia had to be discontinued. When the surgery was over, Dayana lay in a coma, and no one knew whether or not she would come out of it. All that the staff could do was watch and pray. Dayana made a complete recovery and was eventually discharged from the hospital.

The other challenging case involved a young man named Juan. Juan was dragging his fishing net to the riverside when a crocodile lunged at him. The crocodile's jaws clamped down on Juan's right arm. Juan's friend ran to help, and a tug-of-war ensued until Juan's arm was finally ripped out of the crocodile's mouth. Many of Juan's tendons were shredded. Klaus carefully worked away in the operating room on Juan's arm, repairing the damaged tendons and suturing the nasty gashes. Eventually Juan was able to return home to fish again. Without hospital care, the arm would have become infected and required amputation.

In his spare time Klaus continued preparations for Peru. The next step was the purchase of a site on which to build. Klaus had asked the mayor of Curahuasi to find several possible parcels of land. Klaus invited Olaf Böttger, now the chairman of the hospital's German support organization, to join him in Peru in April to select the best plot. As it turned out, they would have exactly ten days to get everything taken care of. Klaus made a list of what needed to be done: form a nonprofit in Peru, purchase land, sign a contract of cooperation with the local health authorities, and negotiate a development contract.

When Klaus went over the list with Tina, she frowned. "Do you really think that's realistic, Klaus? Even in Germany that would be a lot to get done. In South America everything takes ten times as long as you think it will, remember?"

"I know," Klaus replied. "But it's all the time Olaf has, and we have to get it done. All we can do is pray that God will prepare the way for us."

"Then I'll pray too," Tina said. "And if you get it all done, it will be a miracle."

Klaus met Olaf at the airport in Lima on April 7, 2003. He could feel the clock ticking from the moment the two of them greeted each other. Olaf carried with him the $25,000 that had been raised from benefactors in Germany. The men hoped it would be enough to cover the cost of the land. The following day the two men flew from Lima to Cusco and then took a cab for the hundred-mile journey west to Abancay. Olaf had jet lag from the flight and dozed throughout most of the drive. Klaus was too excited to sleep.

In Abancay, Klaus and Olaf met up with John Walter, an American who lived in South America and who was a project manager for Constructec, a large construction company that would build the hospital once the land was secured. Klaus had met John in Quito and looked forward to working with him and Constructec.

Soon after Klaus and Olaf had arrived in Abancay, the mayor of Curahuasi and several members of the town council picked them up. They had selected eight potential building sites for Klaus to look at.

Klaus and Olaf narrowed that number down to two. The other six sites were either too small or too difficult to access. Of the remaining two potential building sites, one was much cheaper than the other, and everyone agreed that it was the better choice. Klaus was delighted they all agreed on the same plot; it was his first choice, too. The land consisted of six anise fields arranged in a triangle on the side of a hill. On the other side of the valley was another hill, and beyond that lay the snow-capped peaks of the Andes. The view was breathtaking.

The mayor informed Klaus that the plot of land belonged to the Catholic church, which was prepared to sell it to the hospital. Padre Tomás in Abancay was responsible for the local diocese's legal matters, and the mayor agreed to speak with the padre as soon as possible.

The next morning Klaus and Olaf submitted the paperwork required by the State Health Department in order to be granted legal operating status for the new hospital. They had seven days to go before Olaf had to return to Germany.

On April 10, Efrain Caviedes, a lawyer from Cusco, arrived in Abancay. He had with him a draft of the legal document that would make Diospi Suyana a nonprofit organization in Peru. The document consisted of twelve pages of legal jargon, all in Spanish. Klaus, Olaf, and Efrain worked through the document together, though Olaf, still getting over jet lag, kept falling asleep. At important points in the conversation, Klaus would wake him and translate sections in the document into German to get Olaf's input.

Two days later, on April 12, Klaus and Olaf signed an initial development contract with Constructec for the hospital construction. At the same time they nego-tiated with Padre Tomás and the Catholic church to purchase the land in Curahuasi, and on April 15 they reached an agreement. The Catholic church would sell the land for $25,000—the exact amount Olaf had brought with him from Germany. Klaus took the money to the Banco de Crédito, where he, along with Olaf, Padre Tomás, Efrain Caviedes, and Allen George, watched as a bank teller counted it. When he was done counting, the teller nodded; the amount was all there. With that, documents were signed and sealed. Diospi Suyana was now the owner of land on the slopes of one of the most picturesque and poorest valleys in southern Peru.

In the seven days since Klaus and Olaf had stepped out of the airplane together in Cusco, they had accomplished all four of their goals without any holdups, bribes, or paperwork logjams. Everything had gone smoothly.

On the plane trip back to Lima from Cusco, Klaus and Olaf completed one last piece of Diospi Suyana business. Before leaving Germany, Olaf had had three professional graphic artists draw up possible logo designs. He had arrived with thirty designs, and between them Klaus and Olaf whittled the num-ber of contenders to ten. Throughout the trip Klaus had shown the ten designs to all sorts of people, from the mayor of Curahuasi to the poor farmers on the hillsides. He asked which design they liked best and meticulously tallied the totals. By the time the men boarded the airplane to Lima, one design was the clear favorite. It was a simple golden sun with a red cross in front of it. "That says it all," Klaus told Olaf. "The golden sun represents the 'people of the sun,' the Quechua people, and the red cross represents God's love for all people."

"It will be a perfect logo for the hospital," Olaf agreed.

Deciding on a logo was the last decision of the first phase. Klaus could not wait to get home and tell Tina about all they had accomplished in such a short time.

Back in Shell, Klaus eagerly told Tina and everyone else at the hospital about the progress that had been made. Roger Smalligan shook his head in wonder and said, "Klaus, I would say you have set yourself an impossible task, but with God all things are possible."

Klaus smiled. He felt exactly the same way.

Now that they owned a building site, Klaus made another trip to Curahuasi, this time with Tina. They needed to find somewhere to live. Tina's parents had given them $12,000 to put toward their own home, and now it was time to find one. Tina and Klaus considered many different houses around Curahuasi before they settled on a place. Its location in the heart of town was its main attraction. Other than that, the two-story adobe house was a wreck: the wooden stairs and railings were eaten through by termites, the windows had drafty gaps around them, and the ceiling was too low—fine for Quechuas, who were normally less than five feet tall, but not for tall Germans. Despite these drawbacks, the house was for sale for $11,500, within their budget. "It will need a lot of work," Tina said, "but I think we can make it into a home."

Klaus nodded in agreement. The place would be simple but adequate. They paid for the house, signed the deed, and took ownership of it, after which they returned to Shell to pack.

All of the John family's personal belongings had to be packed into boxes and suitcases, while everything else was sold or given away. The staff at Hospital Vozandes del Oriente gave the family a stirring farewell on October 19, 2003. Then, four days after Klaus's forty-third birthday, after five years of serving at the hospital in Shell, the Johns were off on a new adventure.

Klaus, Tina, and their three children flew into Lima, where they hired a truck to take them across the Andes to Curahuasi. The twenty-two hour trip was made all the more grueling by the fact that the whole John family was squashed into the truck cab. Three-year-old Florian took turns sitting on each person's lap as the family rolled along over the mountains. During the daylight hours of the journey, the Johns were presented with a series of magnificent scenes, from steep, snow-capped mountains to waterfalls that cascaded down rocky crevices, billowing misty spray into the air. As they made their way along the spine of the Andes, they saw Quechua children hoeing fields on the rocky hillsides where llamas, vicuñas, and alpacas grazed. In the valleys, flamingoes standing on one leg lined the edge of cool, blue lakes.

It was one o'clock in the morning when the truck finally pulled off the Pan-American Highway and onto a sloping concrete street in Curahuasi. Klaus gave the driver directions to their new house.

"Is this it?" Dominik asked as the truck slowed to a stop. "It looks like a garage."

"Yes," Klaus said, pointing at the high metal walls. "It does look like a garage, but behind here is a courtyard and a house—our house."

The dogs next door howled as Klaus undid the padlock on the metal gate and pulled it open. Tina and the children climbed out of the cab, and then the driver backed the truck up to the house. It did not take long for them to unload the boxes and suitcases and take them inside.

"Are we sleeping here tonight?" nine-year-old Natalie asked.

"No," Tina said. "We will sleep at the hotel. Tomorrow, when it's daylight, we'll get started on sorting out our new house. How would that be?"

"Fine," Natalie said as Klaus ushered them out of the house and back into the cab of the truck.

"The Hotel Santa Catalina is just a couple of minutes away," Klaus assured the children.

The next day Klaus arranged three mattresses on the living room floor, and the family officially moved in. The children treated the experience like a camping trip, but Klaus wondered how long that would last once the construction team from Abancay arrived later in the week.

The house needed extensive remodeling. The first thing to be done was to raise the roof and ceilings six feet. Then all of the wood, including the floors, joists, and window frames would be replaced and a new shower and kitchen put in. Within a week, the ten-man construction team had arrived, and much of the house was reduced to shambles. The John family confined themselves to the living room on the ground floor, and except for the mattresses, their only furniture was made from moving boxes. Billows of dust rose when they sat down, and everything tasted of dirt.

Since the construction crew had also removed the doors and windows, all sorts of bugs that none of them could identify flew in and out of the house. Everyone got bitten, and many of the bites became infected. When they all lay down to sleep at night, Klaus could hear the children scratching bug bites in their sleep.

Although the construction crew had promised to be finished with the renovations by the time the John family was due to return to Germany in December, they were only halfway done by that time. Klaus was not surprised—most things took two or three times longer than promised in South America.

Klaus and Tina decided to leave the house half completed and return home. It was time to tell the people of Germany at large about their vision for

Diospi Suyana. How long this would take, Klaus did not know, but he did know that there was no point in returning to Curahuasi without the money and staff needed to move the new hospital to the next phase.

Chapter 11

Sharing the Vision

It was wonderful to be back in Germany for Christmas. The John family moved into the same loft apartment in Wiesbaden that Klaus and Tina had shared sixteen years before as newlyweds. It was cramped back then, and more so now with the three children. Not that they noticed much. Everyone was out and about. Natalie and Dominik learned to ice-skate, while Florian loved to visit Tina's mother, "helping" her with the icing of the *Plätzchen backen* (Christmas cookies). Everyone enjoyed bundling up in scarves and mittens and heading to the Christmas market in the center of town.

With thousands of colored lights set against a backdrop of the old town hall, built in 1610, it was hard to imagine anything more different from

Curahuasi. Klaus loved seeing his children's eyes light up at each new delight they encountered. He was also aware of how precious this family time was. Once Christmas was over, all his energy would be focused on raising funds for Diospi Suyana.

As soon as the Christmas festivities ended, Klaus sat down at his desk to prepare a PowerPoint presentation. He prayed over every photograph and word that went into it. It was vital for the presentation to strike just the right note. The hospital would never be built and staffed unless thousands of people, both Christians and non-Christians, caught the vision. Two weeks later Klaus was satisfied with the presentation he had put together. Yet even as he was creating the PowerPoint slides, Klaus had moments of doubt.

The newspapers were predicting that 2004 would be a difficult year for the German people. Unemployment was about 10 percent, and polls showed that every fourth German citizen was afraid of losing his or her job within the next six months. From a human standpoint, it was not a good time to raise money for a hospital in a faraway land, but Klaus reminded himself that God was in control. If this was God's project, it would succeed no matter how bad the economy was.

Klaus met with Olaf Böttger. The two men discussed their plan of attack to raise the necessary funds. They also talked over the need for a brochure about the project—something they could give to people interested in Diospi Suyana that conveyed it was a serious and credible organization.

On January 16, 2004, Klaus and Tina gave their first presentation to fifty high school students in Frankfurt. The presentation lasted fifty minutes, with the couple taking turns talking about the slides being projected onto a large screen. Although the presentation was a little choppy, Klaus knew it would get better with practice. Besides, the students paid rapt attention throughout. Klaus was sure they were on track—now it was time to drum up as many places to speak as possible.

Ten days after presenting in Frankfurt, Klaus spoke to five people in the living room of a private home in Siegen. The following day he drove to Handewitt Ellund, near the Danish border, to meet with nine people. He would drive anywhere to give the presentation and spread the word about Diospi Suyana. On the weekends Tina and the children went with him, but during the week the children were enrolled in school. Klaus did not worry too much about how many people attended his presentations. He never knew who might be listening.

One of Klaus's larger audiences was at the Evangelical Free Church in Wiesbaden. One hundred sixty people showed up to hear what he was doing. In the front row of seats, Klaus noticed four people who seemed to be paying particular attention: Axel Lantsch, his wife, and their two children. Klaus knew that Axel was president of Stoss Medica, a major supplier of medical equipment to hospitals and doctors' offices throughout the region. Klaus said a quick prayer as he spoke: *God, could Axel Lantsch be a key player in Your plan?* After the presentation, Axel shook Klaus's hand firmly and said, "A very moving presentation, Dr. John. I will help you find the equipment you need. Come by my office and we'll talk about it."

Klaus visited Axel's office on Tuesday. "I've already drafted an informational letter about Diospi Suyana which I will send out to all the medical technology companies in Germany," Axel informed Klaus. And with a chuckle he added, "I put quite a bit of pressure on them, basically telling them I'm sponsoring the construction of this worthwhile hospital in Peru and so should they. I've given them your contact information. Keep me posted on who you hear back from."

Klaus was grateful. Momentum was starting to build. In March, Dr. Kursatz, an anesthesiologist in Wiesbaden, called Klaus to offer him four sets of anesthetic equipment that were no longer being used.

On April 15, Klaus and Tina were invited to the home of the president of the Berlin Chamber of Commerce to give their presentation. The Chamber's president had invited a television producer, the wife of a senior consulting physician, and a number of other people associated with the upper echelons of society to the meeting. Their response to the fifty-minute presentation was enthusiastic. "A fascinating project," the television producer said. "We need to get you on TV—expose you to the whole of Germany. They would love this."

"Yes," agreed the president of the Chamber of Commerce, "but you would have to change just a few things. Why do you keep mentioning your faith in God? I can see that you and your wife have a strong faith, but the truth is that it's going to put a lot of people off."

"I agree," the television producer chimed in. "I just read a poll by *Der Spiegel* that found only 45 percent of Germans believe in God, and just a quarter in Jesus Christ. You have to reach everyone with your message, and if you keep bringing God into everything, it's not going to work. Keep your religion to yourself and focus on the good work you're doing. That's how you will win over the German people and get the money you need."

Klaus looked at Tina. Neither of them spoke.

"Here's another way to go about it," the Chamber's president suggested. "Have two presentations—one for the general public that you could use on a TV show, for instance, and another for your religious friends at church gatherings. That way you could keep everyone happy."

The discussion went on well into the night, and Klaus listened to everything that was said. On the way home he and Tina discussed the suggestion that they tone down their talk about God in the presentation.

As he thought about it, Klaus's mind went back to a book he had read a long time ago about Eric Liddell. Liddell was a Scotsman who had competed for Great Britain in the 1924 Olympics in Paris. He was a dedicated Christian who refused to participate in the 100-meter dash—a race he was favored to win—because it was being held on a Sunday and he wanted to honor the Lord's Day. Not even the British royal family could convince him to change his mind. The British public was angry with him for giving up the chance to win a gold medal and honor for Great Britain. A few days later, Eric participated in the 400-meter race, which he was not favored to win. In the few remaining seconds before the starting gun was fired, a masseur for the American Olympic team slipped him a note that read: "'Those who honor me I will honor.' 1 Samuel 2:30." When the starting gun fired, Eric bolted from the starting block in the outside lane. In just 47.6 seconds he amazed the world, passing the American favorite to win the race and take the gold medal for Great Britain. In the process he set new world and Olympic records.

"You know, Tina," Klaus said, "on the surface they could be right. Talking about God probably will stop a lot of people from helping us, but we need to do it anyway. We need to be like Eric Liddell and openly confess God in our public relations work, even if it causes resistance. He will honor us, and the hospital will be built."

Tina nodded. "Exactly what I was thinking. What's the point of building a hospital if it doesn't demonstrate the love of Christ? Either we build a hospital that honors Christ, or we don't build one at all. God will help us. I know He will. If the people we met tonight don't want to be a part of helping us penetrate the media, God will raise up others to take their place. We have to continue on the path we're on."

By the end of June, Klaus had entered eighty talks into his laptop spreadsheet. Each presentation was meticulously documented: who the contact person was, how many people were present, and any follow-up phone calls or visits needed to be made. Sometimes Klaus made up to seventy phone calls a day to set up presentations, answer questions, and arrange private meetings. Meanwhile, Tina managed things at home, writing hundreds of thank-you notes, honing hospital plans, and making arrangements for Klaus during the day.

Yet for all their effort, the money was only trickling in. In the first six months of 2004, only 251 donations totaling $220,000 had been made. Yes, it was a lot of money, but only a tenth of what they needed. *At this rate*, Klaus thought, *it will be years before we get back to Peru.*

Klaus spent many hours praying that God would turn things around. At times he felt courageous and filled with faith. Other times he wept with exhaustion and discouragement. But there was no way back. He and Tina had declared their belief that God wanted a hospital for the poorest of the poor in Peru. Somehow they had to keep going until a breakthrough occurred.

One day in July, Dr. Gabi Risse, a former colleague of Tina's, called. "I live in Traben-Trarbach, on the banks of the Mosel River, now," she said. "I'm going to set up a speaking engagement for you at my church. When can you come?"

Klaus smiled. It felt wonderful knowing that other Christian doctors were willing to make an effort to publicize the hospital. Gabi arranged for them to come the following month. When Klaus and Tina arrived, they found that Gabi had worked hard getting the word out. There were posters on every street corner and in coffee shops, and a large group of people showed up at the church to hear the presentation. Klaus and Tina were heartened by their intelligent questions.

Two weeks later, Martin Gundlach, editor of *Family* magazine, contacted Klaus. He said that Dr. Barbara Meinhardt, a Catholic doctor from Traben-Trarbach, had written to him suggesting he write a story on Diospi Suyana for the magazine. He invited the John family to meet with him in Witten. If all went well, he assured Klaus, he would write a half-page article for the August edition of *Family*.

When Klaus got off the telephone with Martin, he was optimistic. Could this be the breakthrough they were looking for? *Family* magazine was published quarterly and had a circulation of 50,000, with an average readership of 150,000. This meant that many Germans would get to read about the hospital.

The Johns drove north to Witten, where Klaus and Tina gave their presentation to Martin Gundlach. When they were done, Martin sat in silence for a long time before he spoke. "That is amazing, simply amazing. I want to dedicate the entire issue of the magazine to your hospital."

Klaus was ecstatic. *Yes!* "*He who honors Me, I will honor,*" he thought. Then he had another idea. "Do you think we might provide a flyer that can be inserted into the magazine? It would provide information on how readers could make donations if they wanted to."

Martin did not hesitate. "Of course we can."

Six weeks later, Klaus had an advance copy of *Family* in his hands. Inside, six full pages of the magazine were taken up by a story titled "Doctor's Family Drawn to the Indians." Photos of Klaus and his family in Peru accompanied the story. As he glanced at Martin's editorial, Klaus discovered it was a plea for readers to support Diospi Suyana. Tucked into the middle page was the flyer with the donation information.

As he flicked through the magazine pages, Klaus wondered what would happen next. He did not have to wait long to find out. Within a day of the magazine hitting the newsstands, the phone started ringing constantly. *The Daily Post,* the only Catholic newspaper in Germany, sent a reporter to interview Klaus. *Bild der Frau,* the largest women's paper in Europe, along with an unlikely magazine, *Body and Mind*, also picked up the story. And the major European television network, Sat.1, wanted to interview Klaus. The post office had to begin using an overflow box for the mail Klaus and Tina were receiving. Donations poured in, and better yet, pledges came from people committing to regularly support the hospital. By the end of the month there were another $75,000 in the bank.

Klaus felt the dam had finally burst and things were beginning to flow. More good news was ahead. Pastor Gunter Born from Lörrach, whom Klaus had known as a teenager, called. He came straight to the point. "Klaus, we would love to support you, and though we cannot take on any more missionaries at the moment, we have been praying about what we can do."

"Great," Klaus replied. "Any help is appreciated, especially from an old friend."

Pastor Born continued. "We're going to advertise your mission all over town and then have you come and speak at the end of our advertising campaign. How does that sound?"

"Wonderful," Klaus said. "Give me the details and I'll be there."

On the afternoon of September 28, 2004, Klaus set out on the two-hundred-mile trip south from Wiesbaden to Lörrach, near the Swiss border. He arrived in time to meet with about forty people who had gathered in Pastor Born's church. The presentation went well, and many people gave Klaus money to help with the hospital.

Right after the meeting Klaus drove home to Wiesbaden. The next morning he logged on to the Internet to check the balance of the Diospi Suyana bank account. He had to look twice. A deposit had been made for fifteen thousand euros. Beside the deposit amount was the name Dorothea Kaltenbach. Klaus was intrigued. Who had made such a large donation, and why? He called the bank and asked what city the Kaltenbach check had come from. The answer was Lörrach. Klaus got back on the Internet and typed Kaltenbach and Lörrach into a search engine. In no time he had a phone number for the Kaltenbachs. Klaus quickly dialed the number, and a woman's voice answered, "Kaltenbach residence."

Klaus took a deep breath and began. "My name is Klaus John. My wife and I are the originators of Diospi Suyana. We just received a rather astonishing monetary gift. May I ask if it was from you?"

"Yes, it was," Mrs. Kaltenbach replied.

Klaus hoped she would explain the gift, but she did not. After an awkward silence he asked, "Were you at my presentation in Lörrach last night?"

"No. What presentation?" came the reply.

Klaus was confused. "May I ask how you knew about us, and why you made the donation?"

Mrs. Kaltenbach hesitated for a moment and then said, "I recently read an article about you in *Family* magazine. And there has been talk of nothing but Diospi Suyana all over Lörrach this entire week. I decided it was a good cause and that you would use the money wisely."

"Thank you so much," Klaus said. "I was in Lörrach last night and thought perhaps we had been introduced. You have been very generous."

"You are welcome, Dr. John."

After he put down the telephone, Klaus again typed the Kaltenbach name into a search engine. This time he wasn't looking for a phone number but to see whether there was any other information on the family. Within a few seconds he had his answer. The Kaltenbach family ran an international company that manufactured top-quality metal saws.

Klaus called Pastor Born with the news. "That is wonderful," Gunter said. "Although we were not able to give money ourselves, we did say we would publicize the hospital all over town and see what happened. God is good."

About two weeks later Klaus was headed for Switzerland to give his presentation to a missionary group and realized he would be driving right through Lörrach. He called Dorothea Kaltenbach and asked if he could visit the family and give them his presentation.

Mrs. Kaltenbach did not seem enthusiastic about the idea, but Klaus felt he should be persistent. In the end she gave in and invited Klaus to come by on Saturday morning for an hour.

Klaus showed up at the impressive house with a large bouquet of flowers. Mrs. Kaltenbach opened the door and invited him in. Her husband was there too, along with four of their children. Before long, Klaus felt at home, especially when the children asked him questions about what his own children liked best about living in South America. The Kaltenbach children had so many questions that the presentation took three hours. When it was over, Mr. Kaltenbach said, "That was wonderful. You should come back and speak at my Rotary Club."

"Yes," his wife said. "And at Christmas we usually organize a fund-raiser concert in the evangelical church. Diospi Suyana would be a great cause. Come back then."

Klaus left the house whistling. He was sure that this relationship would last for many years.

Other doors opened with important business-
men. Three months before, Klaus's mother had seen
Ludwig Georg Braun, head of the German Chamber
of Trade and Commerce, on television and suggested
to Klaus that this was a man he should see. Klaus
agreed. Georg Braun was one of the most powerful
men in Germany. Not only was he head of the German Chamber of Trade and Commerce, but he had
also served as the CEO of B. Braun Melsungen Group,
a large pharmaceutical and medical supply company.
Since Georg Braun was not an easy man to get an
appointment with, Klaus asked Axel Lantsch for help
setting up the meeting. In early October, Axel phoned
to say that Georg Braun had agreed to a meeting.

As Klaus, Tina, and Axel drove to Georg Braun's
office in Melsungen, they prayed about the meeting.
Even after praying, Klaus felt nervous. A lot was resting on the appointment, and Axel had told Klaus that
Georg Braun was not particularly interested in meeting with them.

After everyone had been introduced, Georg Braun
asked a few questions. The group talked together for
about an hour, but George Braun did not want to see
Klaus and Tina's presentation. When the meeting
was over, Klaus left feeling deflated. Still, he did not
have time to dwell on it. Many other meetings were
coming up at which he could make the presentation.

True to their word, the Kaltenbachs organized a
Christmas concert and a meeting with the Lörrach
Rotary Club. As a result of the two events, $10,000
was donated along with pledges of regular monetary

support. Better yet, Mr. Kaltenbach had an idea. "What about your hospital maintenance shop? Our company makes saws, and we can supply those, but we know many other companies in similar lines of business. Between us we should be able to outfit the entire maintenance shop."

Klaus laughed out loud, he was so happy. "That would be wonderful!"

"I'll get straight on it," Mr. Kaltenbach said. "I also know the chief editors of the leading regional newspapers. We'll run a series in the press on equipping the hospital repair shop."

Soon Klaus was receiving regular updates from Mr. Kaltenbach, tallying the money and equipment donations that were rolling in. Mr. Kaltenbach instructed two of his employees to work on acquiring and reconditioning the necessary equipment, which he informed Klaus was worth about $80,000. Regular stories on the repair shop project ran in the local newspapers. Klaus was grateful. In the Peruvian Andes it would be difficult to find the proper equipment to fix things at the hospital when they broke. Now the hospital was one step closer to being self-sufficient.

Mr. Kaltenbach also introduced Klaus to Andreas Rummelt, head of the Sandoz Group, which produced large quantities of generic drugs for the world market. Klaus had previously tried to contact Mr. Rummelt by mail but had never received a reply.

Klaus soon found himself sitting in a conference room with Mr. Rummelt and Anne Schardey, director of public relations for the company. Once again

Klaus gave his fifty-minute presentation. When it was over, Mr. Rummelt turned to him and said, "Dr. John, I have to commend you. You communicate a great deal of enthusiasm for this work. What can I do for you? Do you need money? Medication?"

Klaus hesitated a moment. This was an open-ended question. Did he dare ask for what he really needed? He decided to be bold. "Would you consider sponsoring the construction of our intensive care unit?" he asked.

"How much would that cost?"

"Eighty thousand dollars," Klaus replied matter of factly.

"You'll be hearing from us," Mr. Rummelt said. "And I think all our staff would benefit from seeing this presentation, don't you think, Anne?"

Anne nodded. "Certainly." Then, turning to Klaus, she asked, "Do you have time to give your presentation to our 150 employees sometime in the future?" It was the kind of question Klaus loved most of all.

Within days, Andreas Rummelt had transferred $80,000 into the Diospi Suyana bank account. The new hospital would now have a state-of-the-art intensive care unit. And when Klaus gave his presentation to the Sandoz Group employees, the group donated $8,000 more.

Soon afterward, Klaus learned that Ludwig Georg Braun had authorized the donation of hundreds of thousands of dollars' worth of surgical instruments through Aesculap, a division of the B. Braun

Melsungen Group, for the new hospital. In addition, Georg Braun arranged for the ongoing provision of intravenous fluids and medications. Klaus was amazed and humbled by the donation. From what had seemed at the time to be a failed meeting with Georg Braun, God had brought forth an abundant supply of equipment and medicine.

Every night Klaus thanked God for the people and organizations that were giving money and materials for the hospital. He also thanked Him for the steady stream of letters and e-mails he was receiving from doctors and nurses interested in volunteering at Diospi Suyana. In the back of his mind, however, there was one thing that really concerned Klaus. The hospital had to be built—the blueprints had to be read, materials gathered, and workers supervised—by one important person: a consulting civil engineer. That person would have to have a lot of experience on large construction sites, have worked in a developing world setting, be a committed Christian, be willing to move to Peru for two years, and be willing to work without pay. This was a tall order. Klaus had made inquiries and looked everywhere he could think of, but he had been unable to find a single person who fit the job description.

Chapter 12

Cogs in God's Big Wheel

Klaus flipped another page of the fifty-page legal document Constructec had sent him. The document was a draft of the contract to build the hospital in Peru. On February 18, 2005, just two days away, John Walter and another representative from the company would be flying in from South America to go over the hospital plans and the contract with Klaus. And now Klaus was seated at the table in the loft apartment in Wiesbaden reading the contract with Klaus Schultze-Rhonhof, an attorney who had offered to review the papers with him.

"What does this mean?" Klaus asked the attorney.

"Let me see," Schultze-Rhonhof said.

Klaus took off his glasses and rubbed his eyes while the attorney read the section in question.

Wading through all these legal terms was exhausting work, and Klaus knew he should have a construction engineer reading over the papers as well.

"Would you like a cup of tea?" Klaus asked.

"Thank you," Schultze-Rhonhof said. "I think it's time for a break." He stood up and stretched his legs. "You know, I belong to a charitable organization too," he said as Klaus filled the kettle. "There are about twenty of us, and we raise funds for the children of prostitutes in São Paulo, Brazil."

"Really?" Klaus said. "That's wonderful."

"We play a small part in improving the children's lives, we hope." The attorney paused for a moment. "You know, one member of our group used to be an engineer for Philip Holzmann."

Klaus felt his heart race. Philip Holzmann had been one of Germany's leading construction companies before it had gone bankrupt during the economic recession. "May I ask the man's name?" Klaus said.

"His name is Udo Klemenz. He lives in Solms, near Wetzlar."

"You wouldn't happen to have his phone number, would you?" Klaus asked.

Schultze-Rhonhof sat down and reached into his briefcase, frowning as he rummaged around in it. "Ah, yes, here it is," he finally said, handing Klaus a scrap of paper.

"Would you mind if I give Mr. Klemenz a quick call?"

"Go right ahead," the attorney said.

Klaus dialed the number, and a man answered.

"Hello."

"Mr. Klemenz?" Klaus asked.

"Yes, how can I help you?"

"My name is Dr. Klaus John, and I'm meeting with Klaus Schultze-Rhonhof. I believe you know him."

"Yes, I do."

"I'm heading up a project to build a mission hospital in Peru." Klaus stopped and took a deep breath. How would what he was about to say sound to the stranger on the other end of the phone? "We are looking for someone to supervise the construction in the mountains of Peru. It would take a two-year commitment. Can you imagine yourself doing the job—for free?"

After a brief pause on the line, Udo said, "Yes, I could imagine myself doing the job. Can you come by to discuss the project with my wife and me?"

"Absolutely," Klaus said, hardly believing what he was hearing.

"How about tonight, say, seven o'clock?" Udo asked.

"That works for me. I will be there," Klaus said.

Schultze-Rhonhof chuckled as Klaus hung up the phone. "Dr. John, you are just the man for this job," he said.

Solms was an hour's drive north of Wiesbaden, and Klaus rang the doorbell at the Klemenzes' modest home at exactly seven o'clock.

Udo Klemenz, a trim man in his early sixties with a graying beard, answered the door and invited Klaus in. He introduced himself and then introduced Klaus to his wife, Barbara. Soon the three of them were seated in the living room. Klaus got out his laptop and projector and proceeded to give the Klemenzes the presentation on Diospi Suyana. Neither Udo nor Barbara spoke during it, and when it was over there was a long silence. Klaus held his breath. Did they think he was crazy?

Barbara broke the silence. "Thank you, Dr. John. My husband and I are committed Christians, and we volunteer in our local church. Last week our prayer group leader challenged each of us to pray and ask God if there was something special He had for us to do—something more than we were already doing. Udo and I have prayed for three days. In fact, when you called this morning we were sitting in the kitchen, thinking about the direction of our lives and what God wanted us to do next. I believe your call was divine guidance."

Klaus blinked back tears.

Udo spoke next. His voice was strong and certain. "I worked for Philip Holzmann for thirty-five years, thirteen of them in developing countries." He cleared his throat. "I have the experience you are looking for. The timing of your call this morning seems to indicate that God wants us to go to Peru."

Klaus nodded. "It does seem that way, doesn't it?"

The three of them talked for another hour or so. By the time Klaus left the Klemenzes' home, he felt certain that Udo and Barbara were committed to the hospital. He had found the missing piece—an experienced construction engineer—with two days to spare before the executives from Constructec were to arrive.

The drive back to Wiesbaden seemed to take forever. Klaus could not wait to tell Tina what had happened. When he got home, he rushed up to their apartment and excitedly swung the door open. The words tumbled almost uncontrollably out of his mouth as he told Tina about Udo and Barbara. "Udo is everything we've been praying for. He's supervised the building of a large football stadium in Saudi Arabia and a port development in Nigeria. He's been an engineer on construction projects in Libya and many other countries. And his wife, Barbara, will be a wonderful prayer partner for us."

Tina stood silent for a long time, still speechless after Klaus had stopped talking. Then she said, barely above a whisper, "Klaus, this is incredible. You, me, Udo, Barbara—we are all cogs in God's big wheel."

Klaus put his arms around her. "Yes, this is not our project. It's God's, and He reminded us of that tonight."

Two days later Udo joined Klaus and the representatives of Constructec in Wiesbaden as they met to go over the plans and contract. Klaus marveled at how well Udo understood everything that was going on. It was as if he'd been with the project from the beginning.

A month and a half later, on April 7, 2005, Klaus and Udo flew to Lima. Klaus had arranged for them to meet with several key people, including Dr. Roland Kliesow, the German ambassador to Peru; Dr. Pilar

Mazzetti, Peru's new minister of health; Liz Suarez Aliaga, president of the federal state of Apurímac; and Dr. Victor Arroyo, director of the National Council of Evangelical Churches.

On April 15, while still in Lima, Klaus gave the presentation on Diospi Suyana three times to the leading Peruvian newspapers: *El Comercio, La Republica,* and *Peru 21.* Each newspaper then published detailed reports of the project, helping to spread word of the hospital throughout the country. Klaus and Udo then boarded an airplane for Cusco. It was time to head to Curahuasi to show Udo the building site.

Their first stop on arrival in Curahuasi was the town hall to visit Mayor Julio Cesar Luna. "I have some plans on my laptop to show you," Klaus told him excitedly.

"In that case I will call my advisors in so everyone can see," the mayor said.

A few minutes later the mayor's office was overflowing with men, women, and children. Klaus flipped open his laptop and pulled up the plans for the hospital on the screen, along with some renderings of what the hospital would look like when finished. The room went silent as the crowd looked over the plans. Klaus concluded the presentation by saying, "Dear Curahuasinos, it is time. On May 24 we will be back for the groundbreaking, and then we will begin construction."

Everyone looked at the mayor; it was his turn to speak. Mayor Luna stood and opened his mouth to begin, but no words came out. He took a deep breath and tried again. Still no words. Instead, tears began to stream down his face. Someone passed him a handkerchief.

Following the presentation, about two dozen people accompanied Klaus and Udo two miles up the road to the hospital site. Nothing had changed at the site yet, but the two men spread out the blueprints and walked the perimeter of the planned buildings. Klaus fell silent as he looked across the valley at the majestic mountains. A huge task lay ahead, and like his hero George Müller, with his orphanages in Bristol, England, Klaus felt it was important to complete the project without going into debt. So far they had raised $600,000, most of it from small donations. As Klaus looked up at the clear blue sky, he thought, *We have a long way to go. Without God this is crazy.*

As promised, five weeks later Klaus returned to Curahuasi from Germany for the groundbreaking ceremony. Accompanying him were eight medical professionals from Germany, the United States, and Australia, all of whom were seriously considering uprooting their lives to be a part of the founding team of Diospi Suyana.

Klaus had put a lot of effort into publicizing the groundbreaking ceremony, and both the German ambassador and the director of the National Council of Evangelical Churches had promised to come from Lima for the ceremony. The night before, a crew of town council workers had labored to raise a sixty-foot-long stage on a newly leveled stretch of ground. In the morning, the stage was complete, with canopies on either side to shield the dignitaries from the blazing sun. Red, white, black, and gold balloons were everywhere, representing the national colors of Peru and Germany. The day before, Klaus and several others had erected a large sign on the building site that displayed the mission statement of Diospi Suyana in bold, black letters: "With this hospital, we want to honor God and serve His people in Peru."

At two o'clock in the afternoon the festivities began. The German ambassador and the director of the National Council of Evangelical Churches had arrived from Lima and had taken their seats beside dignitaries from Curahuasi and the Apurímac region.

A large crowd began to gather in front of the stage while students from several local schools, dressed in colorful uniforms, marched to the building site accompanied by bands. Churches in the area had made giant posters displaying their responses to the hospital project. One of the banners touched Klaus deeply. It read, "The Diospi Suyana Hospital is God's gift to Curahuasi!"

As the ceremony progressed, the gathered crowd boisterously sang the Peruvian national anthem as their flag was hoisted high. The German ambassador joined with Klaus and the others who had come with him for the ceremony to sing the German national anthem. Then it was Klaus's turn to speak. Klaus walked up to the microphone and began. He talked about how Jesus, at the beginning of His public ministry, had declared, "The Spirit of the Lord is upon me, because he has anointed me to preach good news to the poor. He has sent me to proclaim freedom for the prisoners and recovery of sight for the blind, to release the oppressed." Klaus told the crowd that many people would be healed and cured through the work of the hospital, and more importantly, many would hear the gospel and find spiritual freedom.

Following Klaus, the German ambassador gave an address in which he pointed out that in the future the German staff at the hospital would be working side by side with the residents of Curahuasi. The crowd erupted in thunderous applause at his words.

Dr. Allen George, who had helped Klaus locate Curahuasi as the place to build the hospital, also spoke. He told the crowd how his wife, Amy, had a brain tumor, and although she'd undergone two surgeries, her outcome was still uncertain. "I have learned," he said loudly into the microphone, "that the only things in my life that are of lasting value are the things I have done for God."

Following the speeches, two folk-dancing troupes dressed in colorful costumes performed a number of dances, reminding everyone present of the old Inca culture and the origins of the people the hospital would serve.

Then it was time for the groundbreaking. Various local officials, evangelical pastors, and representatives of the Catholic church gathered around as the first shovelful of dirt was turned on the construction site of Diospi Suyana. As the soil was turned, Klaus thought back to three years ago in Ecuador when Tina had challenged him to stop talking and start planning to make their vision a reality. Now here he was, surrounded by over three thousand people who had caught the vision.

Soon it was time for Klaus to return to Germany. Klaus knew this was the last time he would be going "home" to Germany. In ten weeks' time the whole John family would be moving to Peru—for good. Yet there was a lot to be done. One of the most pressing problems Klaus had to deal with was storage in Germany. As people and companies donated furniture and equipment for the project, Klaus had to find a safe, dry place to store it all. So far, Stoss Medica had allowed him to use a small warehouse free of charge, but now a much bigger space—perhaps big enough to hold ten containers' worth of items—was needed before the items were shipped to Peru.

Warehouse space was not cheap, costing about $3,000 a month to rent. Klaus was loath to spend that much when there were so many other expenses to take care of. He had prayed and spread the word of his need for storage space, but no one had come forward to offer it.

Then the day after Klaus arrived home from Peru, a representative from Stoss Medica called to inform him that the company needed the storage space. Klaus had two days to empty the warehouse. Klaus recalled a phone call that he'd made to Mr. Pfuhl, the director of the Schenk Company. Mr. Pfuhl had told Klaus firmly that their company had no warehousing available for free, but in the end he had offered to let Klaus look at a tiny storage room in the basement.

The room was obviously not big enough, just nine hundred square feet, but now Klaus grasped at the opportunity to meet with Mr. Pfuhl. The next day he drove to Darmstadt, where the Schenk Company was located, praying all the way.

Mr. Pfuhl seemed happy to see Klaus, and he introduced him to Mr. Weg, the custodian. The three men went down to see the room in the basement. It was clean and dry, and Klaus imagined about a quarter of the equipment they already had could be stored there. It was a start. "Thank you, Mr. Pfuhl," he said. "This will be wonderful."

"Just a moment," the director said, holding up his hand. "Mr. Weg, what else do we have to offer Dr. John?"

Mr. Weg smiled and beckoned for Klaus to follow him. They walked through several halls until they came to a large room, where they stopped. "You could have this room too," Mr. Weg said. "And there's an identical one beside it which I think we could also make available to you."

Klaus wanted to let out a shout of joy, but he restrained himself. "How big are they?" he asked.

"Together, along with the other room, they are over three thousand square feet," Mr. Weg said.

Klaus turned to Mr. Pfuhl, who was beaming. "Well, Dr. John, I think we have solved your storage problems for a year, don't you? The three rooms will be free of charge and available immediately."

The problem of warehouse space in which to store donated items had been solved, and just in time.

It was August 3, 2005—departure day had finally arrived. It was also Dominik's ninth birthday, a day Klaus was sure his son would remember for the rest of his life. A large crowd of family and friends gathered at the airport in Frankfurt to say farewell to the five members of the John family and to Udo and Barbara Klemenz. A girl from the church youth group had made a sign with the Diospi Suyana logo painted on it, and another person pressed one last donation into Klaus's hand.

Once everyone had passed through security and gone out to the gate, Klaus relaxed a little. It had been twenty months since they returned to Germany to raise money and find hospital staff, and it had been an exhausting and exhilarating time. Behind them were 173 presentations to individuals, churches, clubs, and schools in Germany and more than thirty thousand miles of driving around Europe. Over two million Germans had heard about Diospi Suyana through fifty newspaper articles and several television appearances. Money had been raised, along with many other gifts of equipment, storage, and transportation. Thirty-two medical personnel were seriously considering moving to Peru to work in the hospital. And now the Johns were on their way to a new life, leaving the comfort of Germany behind.

The building contract with Constructec gave them 540 days—one and a half years—to construct the hospital from the ground up: earthworks, foundations, water pipes, electricity, heating, walls, roofing, painting, landscaping, everything. In the meantime, the medical staff that had committed to serving at the hospital would have to be molded into a single team. They would have to learn a new language or two, as well as how to function in a Third World environment. The three John children would need to be supported as they were immersed in a very different living and educational situation from what they had been used to in Germany. "We have come so far, God," Klaus prayed quietly as the airplane lifted off from Frankfurt. "Please keep Your hand on us. We have so far to go."

Chapter 13

Part of a Miracle

U pon their arrival in Peru, the Johns and Klemenzes stayed at the Swiss Missionary Society
guesthouse in Lima while they checked off the list
of things to be done before heading to Curahuasi.
They all needed visas, and Klaus and Tina needed
Peruvian driver's licenses. They also needed a car
to drive. Klaus soon settled on a used Hyundai 4x4.
It was not the kind of car his doctor friends in Germany drove, but it looked like a reliable workhorse,
and that was what counted in the mountains of Peru.

As soon as their tasks were taken care of in Lima,
they set out on the 650-mile drive to Curahuasi. After
traveling for hours over Peru's twisting, treacherous
roads, they arrived "home." They had a lot to do once
they were there. The renovation work on Klaus and

Tina's house needed to be completed, and Klaus and Udo had to size up progress on the hospital construction site. Work at the site had begun a month after the groundbreaking, while Klaus was still in Germany.

Tasks seemed to move painfully slowly in Peru's mountain regions, especially tasks that involved communication with the outside world. Sometimes Klaus had to remind himself that he was living in the twenty-first century. There were no cell towers in the Apurímac area, which meant cell phones and wireless computer modems were useless. The mayor had the only computer Internet connection in town, and it was via phone lines, which made the connection incredibly slow and inefficient. The town's telephone network consisted of nine coin-operated pay phones. When Klaus wanted to call someone, he had to stand in a long line. Even if a call did go through, there was normally a transmission delay and constant static. Sometimes Klaus had to put down the phone during a call because the sound was so garbled he was unsure what the other person was saying. This all made coordinating the work between the construction office in Curahuasi and suppliers in Lima and Cusco or Olaf Böttger in Germany a nightmare.

John Walter, the project manager for Constructec, kept telling Klaus and Udo that the communication difficulties were holding up construction. Klaus could easily believe it, but as the weeks rolled by, he began to feel uneasy about the lack of progress on the building site. John and his crew had moved dirt around and dug impressive holes for foundations, but there was little other progress—no cement had been poured, no steel fabricated, and no electricity or water had been set up.

One day Klaus and Udo stood on the side of the hill together, surveying the scene. Klaus's camera dangled around his neck. He'd hoped to take some photos of building progress for their Christmas newsletter, but there was none. His mood was glum. "All we have are holes. They have a year and a half to get this finished, and they're already three months into the job. We should be seeing a lot more progress than this. What does John Walter say?" Klaus asked Udo.

"Always the same thing," Udo replied. "Things are on their way. They'll be here next week or the week after. They haven't even given me a copy of the construction plans. There's nothing I can do as a consulting engineer without them. Something just feels wrong about all this," he added with a sigh.

Klaus was a doctor, not a construction engineer like Udo, and if Udo was worried, Klaus knew he should be too.

Later that week several local pastors came to see Klaus with the same concerns about John Walter. They said John did not pay his workers on time and that he was buying diesel in Abancay for much more than he could purchase it locally and then accepting kickbacks from the diesel supplier. Plus every time he stayed in the hotel at Abancay, he was seen in bad company and spotted in several nightclubs drunk.

Klaus was flabbergasted by the accusations. He found them difficult to believe, but he couldn't dismiss them without investigating. If they were true and John was dishonest and immoral, it could sink the entire project. Far too many people had put their faith and trust in Klaus for him to ignore the situation.

Tina and Barbara met regularly to pray for the project, and Barbara specifically prayed that anything that had been hidden would come to light. It did not take long for that to happen. The following Saturday Klaus drove to the construction site. It was payday, and about fifty workers were milling around. Klaus stopped a few of them and asked, "Have you received your full pay?"

They shook their heads angrily. "No. Constructec always pays late," one of the workers commented.

Klaus asked around for John and was told he was in Quito for the week, ordering supplies. This gave Klaus the opportunity he needed. He summoned Constructec's senior engineer along with Andres Murillo, John's right-hand man, and the three payroll administrators to meet at his house at 2:00 p.m. Udo joined them as Klaus grilled the five men on their payroll practices. It didn't take long for them to confess that the finances on the job were a mess. They had not submitted the required paperwork on many of the workers with the state, which meant they were not entitled to any employee benefits, such as disability insurance.

Later that afternoon, Klaus, Udo, and two local pastors met to discuss what to do next. They decided to drive to Abancay and see what more they could discover. It took four days of sleuthing, but eventually Klaus realized that all the rumors he had heard about John were true. Not only that, but also it turned out that Andres Murillo had a long police record and was ripping off the hospital project. Klaus estimated the man had made over $5,000 so far from kickbacks he received on overpriced products and services he ordered for Diospi Suyana. Klaus felt sick. Hard-earned money donated to do good for the poorest Peruvians was going into the pockets of the contractors he had trusted. How much more money was gone?

The last thing Klaus had imagined himself doing was confronting a situation like this, but it had to be done. He called John and asked him to return to Peru for questioning. John said he was bringing a lawyer with him, so Klaus asked the hospital's attorney, Efrain Caviedes, to come from Cusco and join them in the questioning.

Tension grew as the day of confrontation arrived. A binding contract was in place with Constructec that could not easily be broken. If John Walter, who worked for Constructec, did not resign from the job, it would certainly damage Diospi Suyana's credibility. How could they hold their heads up, knowing a Christian hospital was being built by men with a reputation for accepting kickbacks, behaving dishonestly, and disrespecting workers? It was almost too awful for Klaus to contemplate, but he had to.

The meeting between the two groups started with Klaus reading a meticulously compiled list of complaints and observations. At first John sat staring defiantly at him, but his defiance soon turned to deflation. He crumbled under the weight of the truth. When Klaus finished, John wept. "It is true. All you say is true. I will tell you everything," he said.

Klaus took a deep breath. He was glad that was over. Now it was time to clean up the mess. He fired Andres Murillo immediately and made sure that everyone on the job was employed legally and received wages on time, along with all the other benefits the workers were entitled to. Klaus told John that he would consult with Efrain Caviedes to decide what should be done with him.

Three days later, Klaus received forty invoices on which John had changed the date. It was the last straw as far as Klaus was concerned. The hospital had to be free from even the slightest whiff of scandal. John Walter had to go. The lawyers for the hospital and the construction company got to work hammering out the details. They agreed that because of the circumstances, Constructec would be held liable for all financial damage sustained. Klaus was relieved. Not one cent of the generous gifts given to Diospi Suyana would be squandered. Now it was time to pick up the pieces and keep moving ahead with the construction. Valuable time had been wasted, and there was a lot to do in an even shorter time. Udo soon received his copy of the plans and got to work as consulting engineer on the project.

Within days of dealing with the situation on the building site, Klaus received encouraging news. Dr. Roland Kliesow, the German ambassador, had been able to set up a meeting with the directors of Telefon-ica in Lima. Telefonica was a Spanish company that supplied virtually all of the telecommunications in Peru. Klaus was overjoyed when he heard about the meeting. Hundreds of hours of frustration could be prevented if a hospital phone line and Internet satel-lite dish could be set up.

On November 17, 2005, Klaus and Dr. Kliesow met with three Telefonica directors. As usual, Klaus gave his fifty-minute presentation on Diospi Suyana. When it was over, he asked, "Would you be willing to support our project with your technology?"

One of the directors frowned as he turned to a sec-retary taking notes and said, "Get me a map of Peru."

The secretary spread out the map on the table. "Now where is this exactly, Dr. John?" the director asked.

Klaus pointed out the hospital site on the map.

"Curahuasi is miles away in the mountains," another director said. "That must be over six hun-dred miles from Lima."

The first director shook his head and said, "We cannot promise anything now, but we will discuss it and see what we can do for you."

Several days after his meeting, Klaus boarded a plane for Germany, where he was to start a one-month campaign to raise funds and attract staff. Once back in Germany he tried to put the whole construction debacle with John Walter behind him and focus on moving the hospital forward. As usual, Klaus criss-crossed the country giving his presentation.

Constantly traveling and speaking to people was demanding, and on the flight back to Peru Klaus felt weary. The airplane landed in Lima at midnight on December 19, 2005. The only thing that kept Klaus going was the thought that he had only one more flight and a three-hour drive before he got to see Tina and the children.

Klaus had been through customs and immigration in Lima many times before and knew the drill, and thankfully things were moving quickly. He headed for the final checkpoint, manned by two customs officials. Straight ahead was the exit into the public area of the airport, and to the left were scanners and conveyer belts where a group of customs officers were waiting to search passengers' luggage. The system was simple and was supposed to stop corruption. Each passenger pressed a large button before he or she exited. If the light above the button turned green, the passenger continued walking straight ahead. But if the light was red, passengers were directed to the left to be thoroughly searched. Although Klaus did not have anything he was worried about in his luggage, he hoped the light would be green. He was too exhausted to deal with customs officials.

He pressed the button, which turned red. Klaus stepped to the left with his bags. One by one the bags were opened, and several customs officers rummaged through them. Klaus stood by quietly.

"What have we here?" a female officer asked.

"A projector," Klaus said. "I've just been to Germany, and I used it there to give presentations to raise money to build a hospital for the Quechua people here in Peru."

"I don't think so," the officer said, staring sternly at Klaus over her glasses.

Klaus tried to look calm on the outside, but inside he was angry. How dare this woman challenge his story? "Really?" he replied. "I can show you a brochure for the hospital. If you like, I can even show you the start of the presentation I do for thousands of people using that projector."

"That won't be necessary," the customs officer snapped. "Where did you buy this projector? How long have you owned it?"

Klaus explained that he had taken the projector with him from Peru and that he had had it a long time. After all, the outside of the device was quite worn from all the use—it was obviously not new. But no matter how many times he reiterated this, it was clear the customs officer thought he had bought the projector in Germany on his trip and was trying to smuggle it into Peru without declaring it and paying the proper taxes.

It was 2:00 a.m. when Klaus finally exited the customs hall, without his projector. The customs officer had informed him that he had failed to register the projector properly by checking the correct box on the customs form, so she confiscated the device.

Klaus was furious and determined to get his projector back. Right after Christmas, he contacted anyone he could think of who might be able to help: officials from the Ministry of Health; the director of the Council of Evangelical Churches; and finally even Dr. Kliesow, the German ambassador. As a result of their efforts, Klaus was invited to a meeting with the director of customs for airfreight in his office in Lima on February 1, 2006. There he gave the director the same explanation he had given the customs officer at the airport. However, customs still refused to return the projector to him. Klaus suspected it had already been sold and they could not return it even if they were willing to.

Klaus returned to the Swiss Missionary Society guesthouse in a dark mood. More bad news awaited him there. The directors of Telefonica had decided not to help the new hospital by providing a satellite dish and telephone connection. Klaus lay on the bed in his room staring at the ceiling. *What a waste of time,* he thought. *I have so much to do, and I've been running around courting Telefonica and trying to get my projector back, and now I have nothing to show for it.*

After a while he got up and went for a walk to wrestle with his thoughts. "God, how could You allow me to waste so much time?" he asked. "I pray every single morning for You to direct my steps, and this is where I end up? It doesn't make sense, and it doesn't make me happy."

By the time Klaus got back to the guesthouse, he was feeling a little calmer. He had to move forward, and the most sensible thing was to buy another video projector while he was in Lima. This time he would keep the paperwork with him whenever he left and reentered the country. That way he could prove where it had come from and how long he'd had it.

Klaus flipped though the Yellow Pages, looking for a company that sold projectors. There were not many. He wrote down a few addresses and mapped out a route to get to them. Then he grabbed his laptop bag and headed out. He hailed a taxi, which took him to the first address. Klaus frowned as the taxi pulled up to the place, which looked more like a large house than a store. Klaus rang the doorbell, and a young man opened the door and guided him down a hallway and into a large room. Several men were hunched over a long table, working on computer parts. Klaus guessed that they put together equipment as well as sold it.

"Welcome, welcome. My name is Señor Passalacqua. I am the owner. How can I help you?" Klaus turned to see a medium-build man in his midthirties.

Klaus relaxed a little. The man sounded like he really did want to help. "I'm looking for a 2000-ANSI lumens projector. Do you have any?"

"We certainly do," Señor Passalacqua said, guiding Klaus over to a display area at the far end of the room.

Soon Klaus had narrowed his choices down to two projectors. "Do you mind if I try my presentation out on both of them to see which is easier for me to operate?" he asked.

"Go right ahead," the owner said. "What is your presentation about?"

Klaus explained a little about Diospi Suyana and then began the PowerPoint presentation, which he projected onto a large screen at the end of the room.

Within minutes everyone in the room had stopped work and was listening to Klaus. Klaus smiled as he spoke. It felt good to be among a group of positive, interested people again.

One of the last slides Klaus had added to the presentation was of him and the German ambassador making the presentation to the Telefonica directors. As the slide flashed onto the screen, Klaus made a mental note to remove it. The slide served no purpose now. Aloud he said, "That's the German ambassador and me at the Telefonica headquarters here in Lima. Unfortunately, the visit didn't get us anywhere."

As Klaus clicked to the next slide, he heard a voice. "Is that true? Telefonica won't help with such a wonderful project?"

Turning to see who had asked the question, Klaus saw a man whom he had not noticed before standing off to the left. "Yes, it's true. I just received a firm refusal."

"Well," the man said, sounding a little indignant, "maybe I can help. Here is my business card."

Klaus took the card and read it: "Dante Passalacqua, President of IMPSAT."

"It's very odd that you found me here," the man said. "I just happened to be in the area and came to visit my cousin, who owns this place. I don't visit him at work often. At IMPSAT we sell the same equipment that Telefonica does. Feel free to call and make an appointment to see me. And by the way, allow enough time to show your presentation to my staff. They would love to see it."

Klaus was speechless. Here he was, thinking he was trying out a projector, when in fact he had just given the Diospi Suyana presentation to a powerful man—a man who out of the nearly eight million people in Lima was quite possibly the only person who could help with the communications problems in Curahuasi.

Three weeks later, Klaus was back in Lima with his new projector in hand. He had made an appointment to see Dante Passalacqua at his office on the south side of the city. Klaus prayed as he rode in the taxi across town. So much rested on the presentation he was about to give.

Once at IMPSAT's offices, Klaus took the elevator to the fourth floor where Dante and two of his managers were waiting. "Please," Dante said. "Show us the presentation."

Klaus hooked up his laptop to the projector and aimed it at a blank wall to the right. Soon the three men were engrossed in the story of the hospital. When the presentation was over, Dante turned to the other men. "I told you the pictures would get to you." He wiped his eyes with a handkerchief. Then he reached over to his desk, picked up a folder, flipped it open, and presented it to Klaus.

Klaus scanned the papers in the file. "What are these?" he asked.

Dante beamed. "Dr. John, it is my distinct honor to inform you that IMPSAT has agreed to donate a satellite dish to Diospi Suyana and to install it free of charge at the construction site. The equipment will support international phone calls and efficient Internet connectivity."

Klaus was speechless.

Dante continued. "Apart from the installation, our gift is worth twenty-five thousand dollars a year, and we will continue to provide this service free of charge to you for as long as IMPSAT operates in Peru. Our lawyers have drawn up the papers you are holding. They are all legally binding and signed by me."

Klaus sputtered to find the words to say. How had this happened? As a result of his projector being confiscated by customs at the airport, the hospital was getting the exact communications equipment it needed—free of charge for years to come. "This is incredible," he said. "Gentlemen, today you and I have been part of a miracle."

Chapter 14

Madrina

Next to the main hospital building was a sloping area in the shape of a natural amphitheater. Someone suggested they make eighteen rows of seats, walls, a stage, and bathrooms so the local people and the hospital could use the area on special occasions. Klaus thought this was a great idea, especially since there was no movie theater or concert hall in the region. The problem was that there was no money in the budget for something that wasn't a strict necessity. Still, Klaus had talked to local pastors about the project, and soon thirty Protestant and Catholic leaders had agreed to champion the amphitheater.

The pastors had decided to lead by example. On November 11, 2005, they had arrived at the hospital site and set to work on the amphitheater. As the sun beat down, they labored side by side, hauling rocks and terracing the land. Within days word had spread, and Christian men and women began climbing the hill to the site to spend the day volunteering their labor. Little by little these volunteers were building sturdy concrete and rock walls and terraces that would seat at least three thousand people.

When Klaus returned to Curahuasi from Lima with the news of IMPSAT's decision to donate the equipment and services to meet the hospital's communications needs, the amphitheater was nearing completion. On Saturday, April 23, 2006, the amphitheater was officially dedicated. The day had nearly as much pomp and ceremony as the groundbreaking had. This time, though, the people were celebrating the completion of something on which local people had done all the work.

Over three thousand people, all of whom had seats, filled the amphitheater for an inspiring array of music, speeches, and preaching. Then dinner was served to everyone, followed by Klaus and Tina showing the presentation. It was a surreal experience for Klaus. He had told the story of Diospi Suyana in many places around the world and to many people, but never to such a large group of Quechua Indians. As the people sat under the starry night sky against the backdrop of majestic mountains, Klaus clicked the first slide and began to speak. The amphitheater went silent as the image was projected onto a large screen. Everyone, from little children to old people, stared in awe as the story of their hospital unfolded. From time to time when the crowd burst into applause, Klaus and Tina had to pause before proceeding. The people laughed and cried and cheered. This hospital was for them, and they knew it. It was a night Klaus would never forget, especially after such a discouraging few months.

The next morning Klaus awoke to heartening news. The main newspaper in the Apurímac region, the *Chaskies*, featured the amphitheater dedication ceremony on the front page. Klaus was delighted. He could add the photos of the event to his presentation, especially since he was scheduled to go to the United States the following week.

Klaus would be spending four weeks touring the United States and giving thirty-five presentations. He was especially looking forward to seeing Dr. Roger Smalligan, the former medical director of Hospital Vozandes del Oriente in Ecuador. Roger was now living back in the United States, where he had assumed the role of executive director of Diospi Suyana's nonprofit organization in the United States.

Klaus's first stop after arriving was Jenison, Michigan, where Steve Deters, the Diospi Suyana US secretary, lived. Steve was the human resources director for the international industrial engineering company Innotec, based fifteen miles away in Zeeland, Michigan. Steve had arranged for Klaus to give his presentation to the company directors on May 1, 2006. Klaus had actually given the presentation to the directors two years before, when he and Olaf Böttger had made a weeklong trip to the United States to establish the nonprofit support organization, and it had not gone well. The directors had voted not to give any money to Klaus, saying they doubted it was possible to build a modern hospital in rural Peru.

The night before he was to address the directors a second time, Klaus went over the presentation with Steve and his wife, Crystal. The couple was encouraging. "Don't worry about last time," Steve said. "The hospital has come a long way since then."

"That's right," Crystal agreed. "The most the company has ever given to a charity is ten thousand dollars, but if all goes well, Steve thinks you could get five thousand tomorrow."

Klaus smiled. "That would be a wonderful start for my tour."

The following morning Klaus gave the presentation. The directors were fascinated by the progress that had been made and the amount of equipment that was in the warehouse in Germany awaiting shipment to Peru. When Klaus showed the last slide of his PowerPoint presentation—of the dedication of the amphitheater the week before—several directors wiped away tears. "Dr. John, what you have achieved in Curahuasi is absolutely incredible," one director said. "What can we do for you?"

Klaus opened his mouth. "Well, if you really want to make a contribution, you could finance the construction of the hospital chapel." This was the next project on Klaus's mind.

"How much are we talking about?" another director asked.

"I think about one hundred thousand dollars would cover it." Just saying the amount aloud startled Klaus. He wondered what he'd just done. Last night he was grateful for the prospect of getting $5,000, and now he was asking for twenty times that much from a group who had turned him down once before. He held his breath.

"We will discuss the proposal and get back to you soon."

Klaus smiled and thanked the directors for their time, and Steve asked an intern to show Klaus around the huge factory.

At lunchtime Klaus met up with Steve again in the company cafeteria. Steve seemed to be having a hard job settling down to eat. Halfway through the meal he blurted out, "I can't wait for the official notification. Guess what the directors have decided?"

"I have no idea," Klaus replied.

Steve turned to face Klaus and said slowly, "One hundred thousand dollars."

Klaus sat, sandwich in hand, unable to process the news. "One hundred thousand dollars?" he repeated. "Enough to build the entire chapel?"

"You got it," Steve said. "Isn't that wonderful?"

"Yes!" Klaus agreed. "Absolutely wonderful." And it was. The first presentation of the month-long tour had made the entire trip worthwhile. During the remainder of the trip, Klaus flew to the East Coast and then to the West Coast and back again, during which he raised another $30,000. By the time he returned to Peru, he was exhausted, but he knew he would never forget the generosity of so many American companies and individuals.

Klaus arrived in Peru just in time for the presidential runoff election on June 4, 2006. Posters were everywhere, some even painted permanently onto the sides of houses and buildings. The two contenders were Alan Garcia, who had served as president of Peru from 1985 to 1990 during a time of hyperinflation and economic crisis in the country, and Ollanta Humala, a retired lieutenant colonel. When Peruvians went to the polls on June 4, the two candidates were neck and neck. The country held its breath to see which way the vote would go. When all the votes were tallied, Garcia was reelected by 53 percent of the vote to Humala's 47 percent.

Over the days immediately following the election, Klaus had a persistent notion that he should talk to the newly chosen president. He wondered whether ambassador Roland Kliesow could help arrange a meeting, and Klaus called him. A German embassy secretary put him through to Roland Kliesow. Klaus took a deep breath before speaking. "Ambassador, sir, would you be able to help me get an audience with the newly elected president or his wife?"

"Absolutely impossible," Dr. Kliesow said brusquely. "I would not be able to get an audience with the Garcias myself so soon after the election, and I'm the ambassador."

Despite the ambassador's blunt reply, the idea of a meeting with the new president or his wife would not go away. Later that night Klaus e-mailed

Dr. Francisco Contreras, the former president of the Peruvian Society of Ophthalmology. He had met Dr. Contreras three years earlier through the Christian Blind Mission. Dr. Contreras was a member of the upper class in Lima and very well connected. But his reply to the e-mail offered no hope. "Dr. John, I know a lot of people in Peru, but unfortunately Alan Garcia and his wife, Pilar Nores, are not among them. However, I am meeting soon with Dr. Melitón Arce, who served as deputy minister of health under Garcia's first administration. I will mention your request to him."

The following day Klaus received an e-mail from Dr. Arce, and it sounded a little more hopeful. Dr. Arce said that although he did not expect Klaus's request to be granted at such a busy time, Klaus was welcome to compose an e-mail to the president-elect, and he would forward it to him. Klaus responded immediately with a request and some photographs of the hospital construction site.

In the meantime Klaus, Tina, and the rest of the team in Curahuasi prayed that the Garcias would show them favor. A few days later Klaus received a phone call from Dr. Arce's secretary. "Dr. John, you and your wife have an audience with the first lady elect, Pilar Nores de Garcia, on Tuesday, July 4. Dr. Arce will also be present."

Klaus was overjoyed. He felt this would be a very important meeting. Meanwhile, he still had the regular irritations of construction in a developing country to deal with. To solve one problem, Klaus drove to

Abancay on June 22 and returned home late in the afternoon. The drive was always a tense one. Boulders often fell on the road, which had many twists and turns, and vehicles often cut corners rounding the sharp bends.

It was completely dark by the time Klaus reached the outskirts of Curahuasi. Instead of driving straight home, he had a strong urge to check on the chapel construction site. As he turned right and started up the hill, he could make out the silhouettes of three people in the road ahead. As Klaus pulled the Hyundai 4x4 to a stop beside them, his headlights illuminated a man in a floppy hat and two women. Since he had no idea who they might be, instead of stepping out of the car, he rolled down his window. "May I help you?" he asked.

The man spoke. "We are from the Institute of Culture in Abancay. We have just come to take a look around."

"I'm Dr. Klaus John, the director of the project. Are you looking for something in particular?" Klaus asked, wondering who inspected a building site late at night.

The man asked several more questions and then said something that sent a chill down Klaus's spine. "Unfortunately, it seems that Diospi Suyana is not in possession of a license from our institute. Of course, it is illegal to dig in Peru without a license. There may be old Incan artifacts buried here. Who knows, there could be a whole village under this hill. We will inform you in writing what the fine will be for this offense."

Klaus wanted to argue that they had moved almost three million cubic feet of earth and no one had found even a fragment of old pottery, but he bit his lip. Admitting to how much earth they had moved might make matters worse. Instead, he let out a deep sigh, turned his car around, and headed down the hill. He would have to wait and see what happened next.

Three days later an official envelope arrived at Klaus's door. Klaus opened it and read, "We wish to inform you that because you are digging without a license from the Institute of Culture, you must cease construction immediately. Furthermore, you have been assessed a fine according to the table below." Klaus studied the table, which had to do with how much earth had been moved and how deep the holes had been dug.

Grabbing his car keys, Klaus headed for the construction site. There he found Robinson Palacio, one of the Peruvian engineers. "Can you work this out? How much does the Institute of Culture want from us, Robinson?" he asked.

Robinson took out his calculator and punched in a few numbers. Then he turned to Klaus and said flatly, "Seven hundred thousand dollars."

Klaus did not trust himself to speak. The fine was seven times the cost of the chapel that Innotec in the United States had donated the money for. Where was he going to come up with that amount of money?

As he drove home, waves of anger surged through Klaus. Would this be a fatal blow to the hospital?

Could he come up with nearly three quarters of a million dollars? He knew that if he were to offer a much smaller bribe to the Institute of Culture, the whole situation would go away. After all, it had been no secret for the past three years that the hospital was going to be built. But Klaus's hands were tied. He had vowed never to offer a bribe. There had to be some other way to appease the corrupt officials in Abancay. The only thing Klaus could do was pray and ask others to pray alongside him. In an act of faith, he did not order construction of the hospital to stop.

On July 3, 2006, Klaus and Tina left the three children in the care of the Klemenzes and flew to Lima to meet with the first lady elect. Klaus had done his homework for the meeting, researching everything he could about Pilar Nores. It had not taken him long to appreciate the depth of her commitment to the poor. As the first lady of Peru from 1985 to 1990, she had created and directed the nonprofit organization *Fundación por los Niños del Perú* (Foundation for the Children of Peru), which worked with abandoned children. She had also founded and directed the *Programa de Asistencia Directa* (Direct Assistance Program), a government program promoting the economic and social development of women and infants in Peru.

After reading about all of Pilar Nores's achievements, Klaus had a daring idea. He would ask the first lady of Peru to be Diospi Suyana's sponsor, or *madrina* (godmother) in Spanish. This was a serious commitment in which the madrina pledged to support the organization and use her influence to help when any difficulties arose. Klaus thought back to the situation with the container in Ecuador, when customs had refused to let much-needed radiography equipment into the country because of some minor paperwork glitch. At the time, he and Tina had concluded that the way to avoid such situations in the future was to have a patron with close connections to government and powerful people in the country. Would Pilar Nores be willing to extend herself for Diospi Suyana?

On July 4 Klaus and Tina met Dr. Arce in Lima, and together they were ushered into Pilar Nores's office. Every minute was precious. The PowerPoint presentation would take fifty minutes, and Klaus was unsure how long Pilar would let the appointment with them run. Everyone stood when the first lady elect walked into the room. Pilar was a petite woman with long blonde hair and an infectious smile. "Sit down, please," she said. "I am so glad you came to see me."

Klaus let out a sigh of relief. Pilar Nores was just as personable as the newspapers said she was. Klaus got right down to business, turning on his laptop. Then he and Tina took turns guiding the first lady elect through the presentation. Klaus noted that both Pilar and Dr. Arce, who had never seen the presentation before, were engrossed in what they were seeing. The final slide of the presentation simply said in large letters, "Would you be willing to sponsor Diospi Suyana?"

Pilar sat quietly for a few moments before saying, "Yes, I will gladly be your sponsor." Then she added, "Actually, it is difficult to account for the fact that we are here together today, so soon after the election, but my husband asked me to meet with you, and it is very rare that he asks me to do anything. I am very glad he did."

Klaus left the meeting with the first lady elect feeling like all his Christmases and birthdays had come at once. He was certain Pilar was sincere in her desire to help them, and it was such a relief to know that the hospital now had links with the highest political couple in the land. It would make things so much easier.

It didn't take long for Pilar's sponsorship to have a positive influence on Diospi Suyana. Just a week after the visit to Lima, Klaus was on his way to Abancay, accompanied by the mayor of Curahuasi and some of his advisors. Their mission was to deal with the Institute of Culture's $700,000 fine.

The appointment with the institute's director was set for ten o'clock in the morning. As usual, Klaus asked if they could begin the meeting with his presentation on Diospi Suyana. The last slide was a photograph of him and Tina standing beside Dr. Arce and Pilar Nores. As Klaus turned off the computer, he looked the director in the eye and said, "As you can see, the president's wife is in support of our project and has agreed to sponsor us. Do you really want us to stop our building?"

The director paused for a moment. He looked trapped. Then he spoke. "No, no, no, no—of course not. By all means, keep going. Your hospital is a fantastic project. It will bring honor to our region."

Klaus smiled and shook the director's hand. "Thank you. I will make sure you receive an invitation to the opening of the hospital."

That afternoon Klaus ripped up the notice of the fine from the Institute of Culture and threw it in the trash. The president's wife was indeed a powerful ally. Once again, the hospital was on track for completion. Klaus hoped there would be no more holdups, but that seemed improbable.

Chapter 15

Links in a Chain

Klaus looked forward to July 18, 2006, with a mixture of excitement and dread. It was the day the first of ten containers of equipment and supplies was to be unloaded at the docks in Lima. Klaus knew that the half mile from the docks to the front gates could take months or even years to cover. He recalled talking to a priest who had battled for six years to get his church car through customs—and that was with the weight of the Catholic Church behind him.

Still, as Klaus flew to Lima, he was hopeful. Things had been going well. He had just met with Carlos Vargas, the president of Neptunia Inc., a large warehousing and trucking company. After seeing Klaus's presentation, Mr. Vargas had offered to store and transport the first container the 650 miles from

Lima to Curahuasi for free, and later the nine others that would follow. It was a gift worth $50,000.

Adding to the pressure of the container being released from customs in a timely manner was the fact that it contained the tools and equipment for the maintenance workshop at the hospital. The Kaltenbach Company had donated the container's contents, and two of its employees were flying to Peru at the end of July to assemble the equipment.

On July 16 Klaus had received a letter from Pilar Nores confirming her offer to be the sponsor, or madrina, for Diospi Suyana. In the letter she signaled her willingness to help with customs matters. Now it was time to put that to the test. Klaus picked up the telephone and placed a call straight to the director of customs. "I represent the Diospi Suyana Hospital," he told the director. "Pilar Nores is our sponsor, and I would like to request expedited processing of our customs documents. Would you call the clerk at the counter and tell her to accept our paperwork?"

Even Klaus was dumbfounded at how quickly the mention of their sponsor's name sped things along. Ninety minutes later the customs documents were stamped and signed, and the container was ready for pickup. On July 29 a truck belonging to Neptunia drove through the gates of the hospital construction site with the container. People cheered, and Klaus smiled. He wondered if the Neptunia truck driver had ever received such an enthusiastic welcome.

Everyone lent a hand unloading the container, and the very next day the Kaltenbach employees arrived, ready to assemble the equipment and set it up in the maintenance workshop.

By now IMPSAT had installed the satellite dish for the hospital. Doris Bayly, a journalist with the popular magazine *Somos*, along with a photographer, had traveled to Curahuasi to cover the event. The piece Doris wrote for the magazine was three pages long and titled, "Angels of the Andes—German Doctors Turn Modern Hospital in Apurímac into Reality." The article appeared in the September 2006 issue of *Somos*, and within two weeks of its publication, all kinds of wonderful surprises emerged. The first was when a truck pulled up at the construction site loaded with six hundred sacks of cement. Klaus asked the driver where the cement came from. "Guido del Castillo sent it. He owns a gold mine in the south and read about you in *Somos*," the driver replied.

True to form, Klaus immediately called to thank Guido and ask him if he could visit him and show him the presentation. Guido agreed. Two weeks later Klaus was sitting in Guido's office with Guido's sister and some senior employees. After the presentation, Guido asked Klaus, "What else do you need?"

"The next step is the hospital roof. Perhaps you could supply the steel for the roof," Klaus told him.

"We'll see what can be done," Guido replied.

In November 2006, fifty-five tons of steel worth about $70,000 arrived in Curahuasi for the roof. Guido was so enthusiastic about the hospital that he arranged for Klaus to meet with the Chamber of Miners. That meeting resulted in the donation of $50,000 worth of orange roof tiles, enough for the entire hospital roof.

Just before Christmas, Klaus surveyed the effect of the new roof from a lookout point across the valley. The roof tiles made the hospital look bright and cheerful, a landmark that could be seen from all over the valley and surrounding hills. As he took in the view of the hospital buildings now fitted with roofs, Klaus couldn't help but think of all the wonderful things that had flowed from having his video projector confiscated at the airport in Lima a year ago. They were like links in a chain: the surprise meeting with the president of IMPSAT, the article in *Somos*, the cement, the steel for the roof, the tiles. As he thought about it, Klaus chuckled. Perhaps he should go back to the airport and thank the grumpy customs officer who had taken the projector from him.

Klaus received more encouraging news. He had always hoped to have a computerized axial tomography (CAT) scanner at the hospital. With this modern technology, a surgeon could "look inside" a patient and detect many things that could otherwise be seen only by cutting the person open. CAT scanners saved time and lives, but they were also very expensive. Klaus had tried everything he could think of—calling, writing, e-mailing, trying to set up appointments at large medical companies in Germany that he thought might be able to help—but he never received any responses to his inquiries. Then just before Christmas, Tina told Klaus that a Dr. Feldhaus from Siemens in Germany had called to offer the hospital a CAT scanner free of charge. Klaus was dumbfounded. A contact at Siemens had told him that the company had never donated anything as large as a CAT scanner to anyone in South America and never would. Klaus made a note to visit the Siemens headquarters in Erlangen on his next trip to Germany in February.

There was so much to celebrate at the Diospi Suyana Christmas party. By now ten medical missionaries had arrived to join Klaus, Tina, Udo, and Barbara. They came from Germany, Switzerland, and even as far away as Australia. Among them were one doctor, four nurses, one radiologist, two radiographers, and a nursing administrator. Each was in a different stage of learning Spanish and adjusting to life in primitive conditions.

Many of the missionaries had helped with the last stages of planning the hospital, while others worked with Tina to build up the children's club in the area. Tina learned that traditionally, Quechua children worked hard in the fields from as young as three or four years of age. They had little time to play or learn skills that would prepare them to do well in school, and many of the children were abused at home, especially those whose parents drank a lot of *chicha*, a cheap beer made from corn. Tina and Lyndal, a missionary from Australia, had created a kids' club with crafts, singing, and Bible stories. Before long, three hundred children were coming to the club regularly.

As the hospital moved toward completion, Klaus was constantly traveling back and forth to Lima. On one trip in early January, he met with Pilar Nores to finalize the official opening date for Diospi Suyana. It was vital to choose a time when the first lady could be there. They settled on August 31, 2007, eight months away. Klaus also asked Pilar if she would help him get an audience with Eva Köhler, Germany's first lady. He felt that such a meeting would strengthen the ties between Germany and Peru and encourage all the German people and companies who had given so much to turn the hospital project into a reality.

In early February 2007, while he was still awaiting an answer on a meeting with Eva Köhler, Klaus flew to Germany. He needed to coordinate donations and meet with more prospective staff members.

Klaus also wanted to meet with Dr. Feldhaus of Siemens to learn why the company had changed its mind and had decided to donate a CAT scanner. He soon had his answer. Over lunch at the Siemens cafeteria in Erlangen, Dr. Feldhaus explained the company's change of heart.

"I have been director of communications at Siemens Medical Solutions since October of last year. Soon after taking this position I received your letter. I gave it to my boss, Professor Reinhard, who told me to write you a letter refusing to help you. But I could not do it. You see, I too am a believer, a Catholic, and I keep an open Bible on my desk. Your letter talked about your faith in God, and so I went back to ask Professor Reinhard to reconsider the matter. Again he refused, more vigorously this time, saying it was against company policy to make such large donations. Still I could not write you and tell you no. Then

I learned that Professor Reinhard had authorized a large donation to friends of his who were working in Thailand. That was all I needed to hear. I went back and reminded him of your needs, and this time he said yes."

Klaus's jaw dropped open at the amazing story. Klaus thanked Dr. Feldhaus for all his efforts on behalf of Diospi Suyana.

Throughout February and March, Klaus drove all over Germany, making his presentation over thirty times. On March 5 he received the letter he had been hoping for from the Peruvian embassy. It read, "God and all our efforts have borne fruit. It is simply wonderful. It is my pleasure to inform you that you have an audience with Mrs. Köhler on March 20 at 1:00 p.m." That was just fifteen days away, and Klaus immediately called Tina so that she could get herself and the children to Berlin for the meeting as quickly as possible.

Things fell into place, and on the day of the audience with Germany's first lady, the five members of the John family waited nervously at the side entrance of Bellevue Palace in Berlin. They were shown into a luxurious room and told to wait. At exactly 1:00 p.m. Eva Köhler walked through the heavy wooden doors and greeted them.

Klaus and Tina got right down to business, showing the first lady of Germany the presentation. Eva was particularly interested in the role that so many Germans from all walks of life had played in bringing Klaus and Tina's dream to life.

Before returning home to Peru, Klaus and Tina met with several more prospective staff members. In the lead-up to the opening of the hospital, it was essential that they have the right mix of doctors, nurses, administrators, and maintenance workers in place. More doctors and nurses stepped forward, beginning the process of quitting their jobs and preparing to move to Peru.

Back in Curahuasi, Klaus was busier than ever. Many loose ends had to be tied up before the hospital would be ready to open. Some things went smoothly, but even with Pilar Nores at their side as sponsor, they still faced challenges and holdups. One problem was completely out of human hands.

On August 15, 2007, just fifteen days before the hospital was to open, Klaus was in Lima on business. He had just completed three presentations and was walking back to the Swiss Missionary Society guesthouse when suddenly the ground beneath his feet began to shake. Klaus looked up. The power poles were swaying, and the wires hissed and sparked as they touched each other. It took a second for him to understand what was happening—an earthquake! The street began to roll under him as shattered glass fell from the windows. Cars screeched to a halt, and people screamed.

The shaking went on for two minutes. When it had stopped, Klaus hurried to the guesthouse. Everyone was huddled around the television in the common room. The on-screen announcer said the epicenter of the earthquake was 155 miles south in

Pisco. The news from that region of the country got worse as the night went on. Rescue teams desperately looked for survivors. In the end, 510 people died in the earthquake, 1,366 were injured, and nearly sixty thousand people lost their homes. Klaus wondered how this would affect the opening of the hospital. Would the first lady take time out from tending to this national disaster to make the trip over the Andes to Curahuasi?

Bad news awaited Klaus on his return home. Udo told him that Diospi Suyana had exactly sixty-four dollars left in the bank. Klaus felt a knot in his stomach. Had they come so far only to fail now? So much still needed to be done to get the hospital ready to open. He could not think of anything to do but pray.

After several minutes of prayer, Klaus had an idea. He stood up, opened his laptop, and went to the hospital website. He typed in "The Diospi Suyana $100,000 Campaign." He explained that this campaign to get donations would run for three days and would mark the last push to get the hospital ready for the grand opening.

Money flooded in. Three days later when the campaign came to a close, they had met the $100,000 goal. Now they had the money, but they were running out of time. They still had much to do. On August 26 Klaus and Tina took inventory of the situation. Half of the suspended ceilings in the hospital were missing, the windows did not yet have glass in them, and the floors and walls were covered in construction debris. The Johns made a detailed plan of how everyone could work together to make the hospital look as good as possible for the opening. That night they gathered together the one hundred construction workers and their thirty-four missionary volunteers. Everyone got a list of his or her tasks and responsibilities for the next ninety-six hours until the arrival of the first lady, who, much to Klaus's delight, had decided to attend the opening ceremony despite the earthquake.

Chapter 16

From Dream to Reality

When the day August 31, 2007, arrived, Klaus was not sure everything was ready, but it was as ready as it could be. He and Tina made early-morning announcements on the local radio stations, inviting everyone in the area to come to the grand opening of the Diospi Suyana.

By 11:00 a.m. people began pouring into the amphitheater. They climbed the hill on foot or arrived in cars, taxis, and vans. Some were poor farmers dressed in their national clothing, others were wealthy CEOs of companies that had made important donations to the project, and still others were health officials and government representatives. They all sat side by side on the hill, waiting for the ceremony to begin. Flags flew and streamers were stretched above the amphitheater.

Camera crews and reporters from around the country had positioned themselves along the edge of the crowd and on the platform. By noon, forty-five hundred people were assembled in the hot sun, waiting for the first lady and the minister of health, who were nearly two hours late, to arrive. Klaus checked his watch constantly. Just as he was thinking they would have to start the ceremony without them, a cavalcade of government cars turned onto the hospital road at 2:00 p.m. A large cheer went up from the crowd. It was time to begin.

The national anthem of Peru rang out, followed by the national anthem of Germany. Klaus looked around at his fellow countrymen. There was Udo Klemenz, who had so quickly and completely given himself to the daunting task of supervising the building project. Klaus wondered how they would have gotten this far without Udo's experience and steady hand. Udo's wife, Barbara, had been such a tower of support to Tina, especially in prayer, throughout the building phase.

Following the anthems, the speeches began. Everyone from the mayor of Curahuasi to local officials from around the Apurímac region spoke. The first lady's speech drew loud applause. "All of Peru can learn from Diospi Suyana," Pilar Nores declared boldly.

As Pilar spoke, Klaus thought back to the time in Ecuador over five years before, when he had sat night after night for six months drawing up the proposal for a hospital in the Andes. Now here he was, sitting at the opening ceremony of that hospital with the first lady of Peru delivering a stirring speech. It seemed incredible. All the hard work and prayers of so many people had turned a dream into a reality.

Over the next twenty-four hours, Klaus and the other hospital staff took turns leading twelve hundred Quechua visitors in small groups through the hospital. It was an impressive sight, especially to Klaus, who knew how different it had looked just a few days before, still strewn with construction materials. As he surveyed the faces of the people, he smiled to himself. *Some of the poorest among these visitors will most likely be wheeled through these same corridors one day*, he thought. They would be coming for operations and checkups. Lives would be saved, sicknesses would be healed, and, above all, each person would get to hear and experience the message of hope in Jesus Christ.

Many television channels ran reports on the opening ceremony, and articles appeared in all of the large magazines and newspapers in Peru and the surrounding countries. A wave of goodwill flowed over the project. The mayor of San Borja, one of the districts of Lima, sent a letter of congratulations in which she wrote that Peru was not the same after August 31, 2007. Mr. Wawrik, a representative from the B. Braun Melsungen Group who had attended the opening festivities, described his time in Curahuasi as "one of the most impressive experiences of my entire life."

Carlos Vargas, the president of Neptunia Inc., wrote to say that the company would assist in the ongoing transportation of any number of containers to Curahuasi, free of charge. The IMPSAT representative told Klaus that the company would double the bandwidth of the communication satellite dish. Guido del Castillo, the gold mine owner, invested another $50,000 to dig the very first water well in the Abancay province. The well was to be dug on hospital grounds, right behind the amphitheater. Señor Feliu von Josfel donated eight hundred new lamps to the hospital. The list went on. Klaus was grateful for all of the generous donations.

While the official opening ceremony had already taken place, it would be another seven weeks before everything was complete—the suspended ceilings installed, the kitchen and cafeteria set up, and the painting completed. Then the hospital would be open to receive and treat patients.

At ten minutes to nine on the morning of October 22, 2007, an elderly Quechua man pushed through the glass front doors and stepped over the threshold to become Diospi Suyana's first patient. Nearly two and a half years after the groundbreaking ceremony, the hospital was open for business. As patients streamed through the corridors, workers continued putting finishing touches on the project.

"What do you think?" Klaus asked Udo over lunch that day. "When will we be finished building?"

"Klaus," Udo said, "don't kid yourself. A project like this will *never* be finished."

As it turned out, Udo was right. The hospital buildings needed constant maintenance, and new clinics and rooms were already being planned. More importantly, the lives the hospital was transforming both spiritually and physically were open-ended. Diospi Suyana is a link in a long chain that stretches back two thousand years to the resurrection of Jesus Christ, and reaches forward into the lives of children and grandchildren not yet born.

Very Much Alive

You will see when you come to Curahuasi," Dr. Klaus-Dieter John said confidently as we met at Chili's for lunch in Orlando, Florida. "I will show you everything, even the new school we are building."

I (Janet) nodded. I had not yet made the commitment to fly to Peru and make my way to that remote area in southern Peru, but somehow I knew I would. I had met Klaus only twice, but already I sensed that it was pointless to resist his plans.

In June 2013, I flew over the majestic Andes and landed in Cusco. Klaus met me at the airport, and we took the three-hour taxi drive to the hospital.

What I saw at Diospi Suyana cannot be adequately described in this book nor, I believe, in any other. The buildings themselves are beautiful, sturdy, built to exacting German building codes in the midst of an area that appears to have no building codes whatsoever. The orange tiled roofs of the buildings are a beacon of hope on the hillside. Truly, every piece of equipment and furniture in the hospital has its own story. Some of the stories are amazing, and Klaus remembers each one. Klaus delighted in telling me of God's faithfulness in providing everything from the bedpan washer to the CAT scanner to the state-of-the-art anesthesia machines and operating tables in the operating rooms, and from the stunning stained-glass windows in the chapel to the four-ton emergency generator to the electricity-generating solar panels and the hospital elevator for transporting patients to and from the operating rooms.

Just weeks before, the hospital had treated its one-hundred-thousandth patient, whose photo Klaus eagerly showed me. The woman had arrived at Diospi Suyana, exhausted after walking miles from her home village and complaining of crippling headaches. The doctor who evaluated her considered several possible causes. She could have endured many beatings about the head at the hands of her husband. She could be suffering from migraines. She could have a brain tumor. There was no way of knowing apart from giving her a CAT scan—and she had come to the right place for that. Diospi Suyana has the most up-to-date medical equipment in the area. The results of the scan, along with a blood test, were definitive—she had neurocysticercosis, a disease caused by tapeworm eggs settling in the brain and causing cysts. The cysts can block the flow of cerebrospinal fluid, putting pressure on the brain, and can cause a coma or even death. Although there is no cure for the disease, the woman was given medicines that will control her condition and allow her to live without pain or further damage to her brain.

One morning Klaus drove me into the village in his Hyundai 4x4, apologizing that it was not very clean. The vehicle was used for transporting all sorts of things, including adobe bricks that had recently been delivered to help an abused woman set up a new home for herself and her children.

"Helping the woman was Tina's idea, really," he said. I sensed he was talking to himself as much as to me. "It's incredible. When we met at age seventeen, we had the same vision and have worked side by side ever since. Tina is always here for the people. You know, she hasn't left Peru in three years. I spend six months a year in Europe and America recruiting, meeting people, spreading the message, but Tina, she is here. She is the director, the mother, the wife, everything really. What can I say?"

Klaus turned off the highway and added, "Without Tina this place would not exist. I know your books focus on one person's life, but to talk of my accomplishments without Tina's faith and support is not possible."

By now we were in the village. It was the usual mishmash of styles and structures in various states of repair that I had seen in other Third World settings. However, in the midst of the village was a brightly painted, three-story building that housed the Children's Club. Completed in 2012, this is where Tina's work with the children of the village continues to flourish. The children can look forward to something else as well. Klaus took me to the outskirts of town, where I met Udo Klemenz. With a sprightly step that belied his seventy years, Udo showed me around the shell of a new school under construction for the children of the Apurímac region. Klaus told me that when the school opens, five hundred children grades K through 11 will attend, and as with the hospital, the poorest of the poor will be welcomed first.

The school includes the most up-to-date science equipment from Germany. Of course, there is a story to that, as there is to every tile, light fixture, and square foot of concrete that has been poured. Many children and adults in the village are looking forward to the completion of the school's gymnasium. Like the amphitheater at the hospital, it will be available for public use.

"This school will continue to transform the entire valley, just as the hospital has," Klaus told me. "Already young people from this region do not have to go into the cities to find work, since the hospital is the biggest employer here. Over 160 people are directly employed by Diospi Suyana, and we estimate that 100 others make their livings because of it—taxi drivers, snack cart operators, motel owners, all of those people."

On Sunday, Tina drove us down hair-raising bends to a hot springs resort on the Apurímac River.

There we took part in a local church service where a Quechua couple—both in their late eighties—were baptized. Two of the medical staff, John Lentink, a Dutchman, and his German wife, Viola, who live next door to the couple, had started a Bible study with them. The elderly couple became Christians and as a result asked to be baptized. About forty young people watched in amazement as the couple were baptized at the other end of the swimming pool they were bathing in.

Before I left Peru, I sat in Klaus's immaculately organized office overlooking the snowcapped Andes. I asked him one final question, one I was 100 percent sure he would have an answer to: "What next?"

He smiled and stared out at the distant mountains. "Ah, a radio station, I think."

"A radio station?" I asked. "Why a radio station?"

"The people who come to Diospi Suyana often come a great distance—some walk for thirty hours to get here, others take potentially treacherous journeys by bus from the slums of Lima, or they come from the Amazon jungle. But sometimes the specialist they need is not at the hospital when they arrive, and we have to turn them away. If we had a radio station, each morning we could broadcast what specialists we have available for the week—a burn specialist or an ophthalmologist or a gynecologist. You get the picture. It would be much more efficient for everyone. Plus, think of it. We could broadcast Christian programs, health programs, and educational ones as well."

"What would you need to make that happen?" I asked.

"Ah, it will be a challenge," he said smiling. "We would need a modern studio here, of course, and someone to run it and an announcer who speaks Spanish and Quechua. Plus we will need repeater stations to carry the signal over the mountains. But, oh, the possibilities. In a year, about fifty thousand people hear the gospel in our chapel services. With a radio station we could reach at least two hundred and fifty thousand people a day! Our hospital is just a tool, a way of gathering people in. We do what we can. But the real power is in the story of the cross and the empty tomb. I want that to ring through the hill-sides and reach every person here."

Most of the biographies Geoff and I write are of people long dead. I joked with Klaus that a funeral makes a definitive ending to a biography, but Klaus John and his hospital are very much alive. This book ends here, but the story goes on. Today, right this minute, Quechua people are being treated at Diospi Suyana. People from mud huts with dirt floors and no electricity or clean water supply are resting in the comfort of a gleaming, well-lit hospital room. At the press of a button a qualified nurse will appear to address their concerns.

Some of the patients wear oxygen masks, the oxygen coming from a generator located on the second floor and flowing through pipes in the walls to their bedsides. Others have CAT scans, allowing for state-of-the-art diagnosis, like the one-hundred-thousandth patient previously mentioned. Burns are treated, babies are born, and the elderly have cataracts removed from their eyes, giving them their sight back. None of these things would be a remote possibility for these subsistence farmers if it were not for the community of foreign and local believers at Diospi Suyana who, led by Klaus and Martina John, have given the best they have to make it possible.

To follow the ongoing work of Diospi Suyana, see photos of the hospital, and read stories of the people who have been treated, go to *diospi-suyana* .*com* (the website is available in English, German, and Spanish).

Janet Benge

Bibliography

Boyes, Eleanor. *Bridge to the Rain Forest: Medical Missions at the Jungle's Edge.* Colorado Springs: World Radio Missionary Fellows, 1995.

John, Klaus-Dieter. *Dios es visible: Una conmovedora historia sobre la fe en acción.* Miami: Editorial Vida, 2012.

Janet and Geoff Benge are a husband and wife writing team with more than thirty years of writing experience. Janet is a former elementary school teacher. Geoff holds a degree in history. Originally from New Zealand, the Benges spent ten years serving with Youth With A Mission. They have two daughters, Laura and Shannon, and an adopted son, Lito. They make their home in the Orlando, Florida, area.

Also from Janet and Geoff Benge...
Christian Heroes: Then & Now

More adventure-filled biographies for ages 10 to 100!

Isobel Kuhn: On the Roof of the World • 978-1-57658-497-2
Elisabeth Elliot: Joyful Surrender • 978-1-57658-513-9
Paul Brand: Helping Hands • 978-1-57658-536-8
D. L. Moody: Bringing Souls to Christ • 978-1-57658-552-8
Dietrich Bonhoeffer: In the Midst of Wickedness • 978-1-57658-713-3
Francis Asbury: Circuit Rider • 978-1-57658-737-9
Samuel Zwemer: The Burden of Arabia • 978-1-57658-738-6
Klaus-Dieter John: Hope in the Land of the Incas • 978-1-57658-826-2

Available in paperback, e-book, and audiobook formats.
Unit Study Curriculum Guides are available for select biographies.
www.ywampublishing.com

CHRISTIAN HEROES: THEN & NOW are available in paperback, e-book, and audiobook formats, with more coming soon!

www.HeroesThenAndNow.com